Coward and Company

Coward and Company

RICHARD BRIERS

 Robson Books

The author and publishers wish to thank *Punch* magazine for permission to reproduce drawings from reviews of Noël Coward's plays

First published as paperback in Great Britain in 1999 by Robson Books, 10 Blenheim Court, Brewery Road, London, N7 9NT
First published in Great Britain in 1987 by Robson Books Ltd.

British Library Cataloguing in Publication Data
A catalogue record for this title is available from the British Library

ISBN 1 86105 232 4

Printed in Great Britain by WBC Book Manufacturers Ltd, Mid-Glamorgan, South Wales

Contents

Introduction

'I INTEND TO travel through life first class,' declared Noël Coward. Armed with enormous energy and determination and backed by an ambitious mother, the small boy from Teddington set out to achieve his goal.

He was precocious, pushy and assertive, already conscious of an enormous latent talent. A love of words, together with a highly sensitive ear, enabled him in later years to write his brilliant lyrics and enchanting songs; and it was these songs which first made me aware of his enormous talent when I heard him singing them on the radio.

To me, as to so many other people, he appeared to live in another stratosphere; for all we knew he could have been on Mars. As a result, when you did finally meet him, the aura that surrounded Noël Coward was quite overpowering.

I remember an occasion when he collected my wife to give her a lift from one theatre to another and turned up in an Austin Princess – the sort of limousine fitted with rugs and seats that fold down that I always associate with frightfully grand people like mayors.

'I suppose you expected a Rolls-Royce,' said Coward to poor Annie, who was in enough of a state of bewilderment as it was.

'Well . . . I suppose, I always seem to think of you in a Rolls-Royce,' she stumbled in reply. To which

Coward answered imperiously, 'Very unfashionable, you know. Terribly non-U. Austin Princesses are now in.'

We both found his presence quite overwhelming.

When I was in Tom Stoppard's play *The Real Inspector Hound*, Coward came round and sat in the very dressing-room that he'd occupied himself when he'd played *Design For Living* with Alfred Lunt and Lynn Fontanne. I'm still hopelessly star-struck today, and on that occasion in Coward's presence I was completely tongue-tied.

I tried offering him a drink.

'Vodka and tonic,' he replied. I hadn't any vodka.

I nipped next door to Ronnie Barker. 'I've only got half a bottle,' he warned – and that was a shade optimistic when I looked at the level.

Then I found I didn't have a decent glass, so Coward had to make do with an awful tooth-mug of a tumbler.

Dithering about in a lather of perspiration, I tried to be self-deprecating and said to him of the play, 'Of course this is just a light romp, sir.'

'I really think it's a little more than that,' he replied crisply. And he was absolutely right: it's a very clever play. Again I'd been wrong-footed, neatly and precisely – as only the Master knew how.

Set against this devastating effect he could have on us lesser mortals was his universal charm, a quality that seemed to characterize the theatre of his day and which Coward's work brought to the stage in his own performances and in those of fellow stars, notably Gertrude Lawrence.

Not that Noël Coward necessarily had it all his own way as a playwright. He had written several early flops when his first serious play, *The Vortex*, was produced.

This tackled the subject of drug addiction and shocked the conservative audiences of the day. In fact, on leaving the stage-door after the first night, he was spat at. The effect of *The Vortex* must have been very similar to the effect that *Look Back in Anger* had later.

His writing went from strength to strength, culminating in three plays: my favourite, *Private Lives; Present Laughter*, in which he wrote himself a fine star vehicle as Garry Essendine; and, of course, *Hay Fever*.

With the arrival of kitchen-sink drama, the charm and glamour of Noël Coward's world was eclipsed by a greyer cloud of realism ('a terrible pall of significance' he once called it). His work became unfashionable and he was regarded by several critics as a has-been who wrote clever, rather shallow plays. This naturally hurt him a great deal, but as he often said in times of adversity, 'Press on, dear boy, press on.'

This he did by creating his fabulous cabaret act which took Las Vegas by storm. I'm never entirely certain that Coward was a great actor, and I don't really think he thought so either. But anyone listening to the record of his Las Vegas show can never doubt that he was a great performer.

It was a happy chance that he lived long enough to see his work reappraised, and to see the inevitable swing away from plays dealing solely with the problems and miseries of the human condition.

Audiences were dying to be touched again. They wanted to care about the people on stage, not just to be shocked by their behaviour. The rediscovery of plays like *Private Lives* and *Present Laughter* brought that charm back to the theatre, and some of it rubbed off on television – as we discovered to our delight with *The Good Life*.

In Coward's own case, what no audience ever saw was the single-minded quest for perfection which coloured all his work; the hours of meticulous rehearsal that went into polishing and perfecting the tiny details of each exquisite performance.

The Las Vegas show is a very good example. When, several years after his appearance at the Desert Inn, the idea was put to Coward that he might revive part of it for a televison show, he dismissed it politely, but firmly, commenting that those asking clearly had no idea how long it would have taken him to resuscitate and re-rehearse that material. And when you listen to the recording of that brilliant show, with all the lines to be learnt, and you notice the absolute precision of his timing, you begin to appreciate the endless hours of rehearsal that he must have devoted to concealing his art beneath a veneer of effortless ease.

Coward's industry and sense of professionalism were immense and in this I've always found him an awesome but inspiring example. For instance, Coward would always arrive for the first day of rehearsal knowing all his words – and knowing them well. I also know mine – badly. By the same token I can't polish up a performance as quickly as he could, but I do try to be a step ahead: middle-aged actors tend to get more nervous!

I like to think I've learned something of the precision of light comedy from him as well. But most importantly has been his lesson in the sheer hard work involved in playing comedy successfully – especially when it comes to mastering his own plays, as I discovered when I set about learning the part of Roland Maule in *Present Laughter*.

Noël Coward's declining years were dogged by

ill-health. 'Curse my ageing body,' he would say. But the time was made bearable by the love and respect that surrounded him at home and all over the world.

His seventieth birthday was marked by seven days of parties and receptions, ending with an evening of excerpts from his work performed by hundreds of stars at the Phoenix Theatre, where he and Gertie Lawrence had enjoyed their legendary success in *Private Lives*. The adulation was at its height; almost overwhelming. With characteristic wit and levelheadedness Noël called the seven-day bonanza 'Holy Week'.

Even at the pinnacle of his fame his feet remained firmly planted on the ground, as they had done throughout the remarkable career that I have tried to recall in the pages that follow through anecdotes and recollections of both the Master himself and of his friends on and off the stage.

Don't put your daughter on the stage, Mrs Worthington

NOËL COWARD ALWAYS wanted to go on the stage – or at least he did by the time Lila Field cast him as Prince Mussel in her play for children, *The Goldfish*. At the first rehearsal the very young Micheal MacLiammoir asked tentatively of the disarmingly mature Coward, 'What are you going to be when you grow up?'

'An actor, of course,' he replied with absolute certainty and characteristic verbal precision. He was ten years old at the time and in this case the child was very definitely father of the man.

Nine months later he got his first taste of the adult stage in Sir Charles Hawtrey's production of *The Great Game*, in which he was given a one-line walk-on part as a page-boy in the last act. He made his first appearance at the dress rehearsal and delivered the line with such full-blown confidence, pregnant with innuendo and nuance, that Hawtrey was heard telling his stage-manager (who had engaged Coward for the part), 'Tarver, never let me see that boy again.'

Good nature and the pending opening caused him to relent, though in the ensuing run he saw more of the young actor than he cared for. 'Keep away from me boy,' he used to tell his little shadow, who extorted seventeen autographs before Hawtrey gave up signing the book covered with a design of sweet peas. He also banned him from the wings after Coward's chattering once made him miss an entrance.

But Coward was eager to learn from an actor whose talent he instinctively recognized, even at the age of eleven, and for his part Hawtrey offered valuable lessons. (He got Coward to deliver his one line in a Cockney accent, more in keeping with the part than his polished chorister tones, and rewarded him with an extra entrance.)

Hawtrey also possessed a natural sense of style which Coward can only have envied. Unlike his successful protégé, Sir Charles Hawtrey spent the best part of his life hovering on the border-line of debt, usually redder than black. This led him to develop strategies for dealing with creditors and their agents, which included his masterly reception of one writ-server, who was greeted with utmost civility, offered a cigar and asked whether he was doing anything that evening. On hearing that he had no specific plans, Hawtrey insisted that he should be his guest in his current play, disappeared into his office, called his secretary and returned a moment later with an envelope saying, 'There you are, my dear chap, two for tonight'.

Overwhelmed by this unaccustomed courtesy, the writ-server mumbled words of thanks and left. His reaction on finding his writ inside the envelope when he opened it some time later can be imagined!

From Lady Hawtrey, too, the young Coward must have developed appreciation of the well-turned phrase and effortless bon mot. Recovering from a spell in hospital the lady answered a nurse's knock at her door with, 'Come in. Friend or enema?' Echoes of this are heard in Coward's own medical dealings. Before appearing in *Our Man in Havana*, the film company took out insurance on him which required a medical examination. An appointment was duly made with the company's doctor, who was summoned to meet Coward at the Savoy. There he examined the Master from head to foot and ended by asking for a urine sample.

'No, no,' he was told. 'It's really out of the question. Quite impossible.'

'Just a teaspoonful?'

'I haven't a teaspoon on me,' said Coward, showing him the door.

To his own doctor, who once confessed that he had lapses of memory – 'lacunae' to use his own terminology – Coward thereafter delivered the greeting, 'Ah, here comes the Lily of Lacunae.'

From the Hawtrey stable the precociously talented boy actor progressed a couple of years later to the part of Slightly in J.M. Barrie's eternal classic *Peter Pan*, which played at The Duke of York's Theatre at Christmas 1913. Looking back, Ken Tynan was moved to observe, 'Forty years ago he was Slightly in *Peter Pan* and you might say he has been wholly in *Peter Pan* ever since.'

Contemporary critics were more charitable and offered words of warm praise for the new recruit, who went on to tour with the production in the early months of 1914. Heading the cast was the American actress Pauline Chase, who'd taken over Peter from Nina Boucicault and had been playing it ever since the very first tour.

As well as its obvious dramatic success, this first tour of Barrie's most popular play was notable for the cast's addiction to golf, actively fostered by the playwright. For some reason Sir James had got it into his head that the surest way of preserving the physical and maybe moral welfare of the company was to have them striding the links and fairways of the country. To this end he inaugurated and sponsored the Peter Pan Golf Club, which offered a variety of trophies and the not inconsiderable inducement of a prize fund of over £500.

Pauline Chase was elected the club's first president while the company were train-bound for Scotland – appropriately. The actor playing Smee was made captain, since he seemed to be the only member of the 'club' who'd actually set foot on a golf course.

Not dissuaded, the committee awarded handicaps: fifty to Miss Chase in deference to her status as president; forty to the other ladies; and twenty-five to the gentlemen, excepting A.E. Matthews who was foolish enough to let slip the golfing term 'brassie' and who was also the victim of the malicious gossip that he'd been known to hit a golf ball from a tee. He was given a handicap of Plus 2.

On Barrie's instructions the company was kitted out with the finest clubs and equipment that Edinburgh could provide and a special baggage wagon was assigned to convey the forty leather golf bags, all inscribed PPGC, around the country.

It was just a pity that when put to use even these superb accoutrements were unable to raise the standard of play. At Troon, great clouds of the hallowed turf were sent flying, club shafts snapped and balls stayed resolutely unmoved. Further south, the PPGC were warned never to return to courses at Leeds and Newcastle. Unbowed, the company pressed ahead, spurred on no doubt by their president's announcement that if she won a competition the producer, Charles Frohman, had promised to take the whole show to Paris. A hasty reconvening of the handicap committee ensured her triumph, which was saluted in the French capital by one and all drinking champagne from the Frohman Cup.

Barrie switched tracks after that and the cast of *Peter Pan* found themselves taking on local French teams – at cricket, another of the author's passions.

In its early days *Peter Pan* was doing as good business with adult audiences in the evenings as it was with matinée houses full of children. The play always brought pleasure to every age group. During Joan Greenwood's spell as Peter, Hermione Gingold joined the audience for one performance and made her own small contribution to the evening's entertainment. 'Do you believe in fairies?' Peter asked the house, in the scene where he saves the life of Tinkerbell. '*Believe* in them, darling?' answered the unmistakable Gingold tones. 'I know *hundreds* of them!'

Gladys Cooper, another of Noël Coward's fellow players had for many years mixed views about the play, and certainly about mixing the fantasy of the stage with the fact of the dressing-room. After one of her matinées as Peter a small boy was brought round to meet her. He eyed the actress with suspicious silence for some time and then said, 'Well, now fly.'

There's not a great deal you can say to a request like that.

From Barrie's classic Coward moved off through a succession of contemporary plays over the next four years, playing in London theatres while bombs fell from Zeppelins and touring the provinces, soaking up stage life and stage craft.

The summer of 1919 found him playing Ralph in

Beaumont and Fletcher's play *The Knight of the Burning Pestle*, the only piece from the golden age of Elizabethan theatre in which he ever became embroiled; that single taste of Beaumont and Fletcher was probably enough for him.

His enthusiasm can't have been boosted by the response of at least one influential member of the audience, the formidable Mrs Patrick Campbell. Coward had not long made her acquaintance when he appeared as Ralph and he was no doubt flattered when she rang him to ask for a box at one of the matinées. This Coward provided, only to be rewarded by the sight of his illustrious guest snoring away quite unabashed fairly early on in the play. The polite but hardly exuberant applause at the end roused her from her siesta.

Coward, furious and fearless, sent a message via a friend ticking off the great lady and suggesting that the least she could have done was to have been a little more discreet in taking her nap. The message didn't go unheeded. The next night he went on, there was Mrs Pat prominently seated in the house and clad in white gloves the full length of her arms, applauding every line he spoke!

In pieces in which he felt more at home audiences were rapidly warming to the new rising star of the London stage, and when his own plays started to match Coward the actor with Coward the dramatist the theatrical world was electrified.

The Vortex, which opened at the Everyman Theatre in Hampstead in November 1924 before its highly successful transfer to the West End a month later, had them spellbound. Noël Coward took the part of the drug dependent Nicky Lancaster and, in the words of

James Agate's glowing review, 'lived the part with his nerves and was so life-like that you seemed to be in the same room with him'. Lessons learned in Hawtrey's presence were paying off.

Friends saw other sides of this memorable performance. Sybil Thorndike remembers the hysteria he brought to the part, on and off the stage. During the run, she spotted him one day riding ahead of her in an open taxi down Sloane Street. From their old car, she and Lewis Casson, her husband, created a terrific din to try to attract Coward's attention. He failed to recognize them and finally exploded into a horrifying scream of 'Stop it! Stop it!'

Another young hopeful, John Gielgud, also grew to appreciate the psychological demands that Coward had created in Nicky Lancaster; as Coward's successor in the part, he got his first 'smart' taste of the West End. Apparently he'd been offered the part because he could play the piano a little. Meeting Coward at the Royalty Theatre, in a dressing-room complete with scent bottles and a phalanx of dressing-gowns, was a daunting experience for the young actor, who had been pursuing an altogether less colourful career on the Oxford Stage.

He took over the part a few weeks after that first meeting and the production transferred to the Little Theatre, where Gielgud gave a graphic display of the same nervous tension that had had the author screaming his way down Sloane Street. A cat sauntered on to the stage one night, during the climactic last act. This threw Gielgud into hysterics and the animal was summarily thrown into the audience which, luckily for the cat, was sitting almost level with the stage, affording it a relatively gentle landing and the chance to slink away – vowing to stick to pantomime ever after, no doubt!

That autumn Broadway welcomed Coward's Nick Lancaster with such a din of enthusiasm that when the curtain fell on the first act of the opening night the cheering was so tumultuous that the cast of a play being staged two blocks away came out and took bows on the strength of it!

A year later London was almost as ecstatic at his portrayal of Lewis Dodd in *The Constant Nymph* though here again Mrs Patrick Campbell took a different line. Pleading poverty this time, she persuaded Coward to let her into a dress rehearsal and then telephoned after the performance to tell him he was the wrong type, had no glamour and ought to wear a beard.

Once more it was John Gielgud who succeeded Coward in the lead, again on the modest admission of his piano tinkling. Edna Best played opposite him and, whatever Mrs Pat's reaction to the production, that great lady of the theatre Madge Titheradge was visibly moved – so moved, in fact, that she fainted in Edna Best's dressing-room after coming round to congratulate her. But then, according to Sir John Gielgud, she made rather a habit of fading away on and off stage. He remembers her slipping from consciousness at the end of the second act of *Theatre Royal* a few years later, sinking to the boards as the curtain came down.

Noël Coward had an enormous respect for Miss Titheradge, who was to appear in two of his other plays: *Home Chat* and *The Queen Was in the Parlour*. This was an admiration bred from a youthful infatuation. A decade or more earlier, she was leaving the theatre when a boy of fourteen came up to offer her a bunch of rather faded flowers gripped in his hot hand. She

STRAINED RELATIONS-IN-LAW.

Mrs. Ebony . . Miss Henrietta Watson.
Mrs. Chilham . Miss Nina Boucicault.

accepted them, asking whether his parents knew that he had come to speak to her.

'No,' he answered, shy and not a little frightened.

'What's your name?' she asked.

'Noël Coward,' he replied.

In the intervening years growing self-confidence and a marvellous feeling for the stage had worked quite a transformation. An example of this was one occasion during the run of *The Constant Nymph* when Elissa Landi missed a cue and it fell to Coward and Cathleen Nesbitt to save the day.

The crisis came at a moment of high drama, as the two of them were rowing furiously and approaching the point when Miss Landi should have stormed on stage to stop their verbal scrapping. The cue was given, but no Miss Landi appeared. Coward and Cathleen Nesbitt kept the row going for as long as they could until he suddenly broke off, saying, 'I'm not going to speak to you any more. It just isn't worth it!' and, striding across to the piano, sat down to play.

By now Elissa Landi was seized with the terrible knowledge that she should have been on stage and, rushing to the wings, mistook the fireplace for the door beside it and came on like a rather elegant Father Christmas right through it. From the piano stool, Coward caught a glimpse of a pair of shapely legs coming down the chimney and instinctively hit a series of resounding chords which drew the audience's attention while Elissa Landi slipped on stage late, but unnoticed.

A year later Noël Coward was back on the West End boards playing Clark Storey in S.N. Behrman's play *The Second Man*. The intervening period had been a trying one. Two of his own plays, *Home Chat* and

Sirocco, had been booed off the London stage within the space of four weeks and many of the critics were baying for blood.

In spite of this, Coward arrived at the first rehearsal calm, confident and word perfect, as was his wont – to the alarm of most actors who ever acted with or for him.

The fact that his part in Behrman's play was getting on for the length of Hamlet didn't make the other members of the cast, still glued to their books, feel any easier – especially Zena Dare, who'd been cast as his wealthy and sophisticated mistress. She spent the first days of rehearsing in tears until Coward took her aside and offered a few gentle words on self-discipline. 'Now look, Zena. You can't go on like this. After all, if you were working for the Post Office you couldn't go on like this, could you?' And he suggested working on their scenes together in private.

Come the first night, there were other words of encouragement. As they emerged from their dressing-rooms for the first call, Coward took one look at his leading lady and remarked, 'Well, if you look like *that* it doesn't matter how you play the part.' This boosted her confidence no end at the time, although on reflection she wasn't quite sure how to take it.

There was certainly no doubt about Coward's own performance. After the second night, Hannen Swaffer, who as theatre critic for the *Daily Express* had been one of the most abusive attackers of Coward's recent failures, went round after the show to tell him, 'Noley, I've always said you could act better than you write.'

'And I've always said exactly the same about you,' was Coward's instant retort.

His next West End appearance set the seal on a

dramatic career from which, as an actor and play-wright, there was no looking back. This was his portrayal of Elyot Chase in *Private Lives*, which arrived from an out-of-town try-out in Edinburgh in the summer of 1930.

Opposite him in the play's other major part was Gertrude Lawrence, who for seventeen years had been his favourite actress ever since their first meeting at the Liverpool Rep when they were both in their early teens.

She was the perfect foil for Coward's own performance and so confident were they both of the play's success that they split the costs three ways with the producer C.B. Cochran to ensure a handsome return from the box office. They weren't to be disappointed.

All the same, Miss Lawrence wasn't the easiest actress to work with, though Noël had the measure of her. He used to say that she was on to a part so quickly that she shouldn't be allowed back into the theatre between the first reading and the opening night. He also knew exactly how to deal with the range of moods she would don. 'What is it to be this morning, dear?' he would greet her. 'Duchess day; gamine day; or just plain-Jane-and-no-nonsense day?'

Others had to learn how to cope with the mercurial star by trial and error. Six years earlier Jessie Matthews, then a sylph-like seventeen, had been Gertrude Lawrence's understudy in *André Charlot's Revue of 1924* on Broadway. Among the numbers sung by Miss Lawrence was Coward's 'Parisian Pierrot', which he'd written specifically for her in his own revue *London Calling!*

She had never been very taken with it, however, and

while they were playing in New York suggested that the young understudy might do it instead. Jessie Matthews was certainly well able to cope with the challenging range of the song; what she had to learn to cope with was an unpredictable leading lady.

On a number of occasions Miss Lawrence's dresser would bring the Pierrot costume upstairs for Jessie to change into, only to reappear when she was fully dressed to say that the star had changed her mind and was going to do the number herself. Not only was this very distracting for Jessie, it meant that she also lost her normal position in the chorus; as its leader, it was her perk to be last off, so taking the bow in the spotlight and getting the applause. Eventually, this happened once too often for the understudy's liking and she told Gertie's dresser that if it happened in future she wasn't going to get out of the costume once she was dressed.

The next night the change of heart came as regularly as clockwork, but Jessie Matthews stuck to her guns, told the dresser that now she was changed she was going on and went down to the wings to make her entrance as the Pierrot.

Gertrude Lawrence laughed when she was told what had happened. She knew all about understudying herself.

Although the success of *Private Lives* rested largely with the two principals, Coward was careful not to weaken its impact by casting actors who weren't up to carrying the other parts. He picked the delightful Adrienne Allen to play Sybil, while a young and dashing actor named Laurence Olivier was given the part of Victor Prynne. Both of them made plausible, if ultimately inadequate, partners for Elyot and Amanda.

The four of them had enormous fun during the long runs in London and New York, although the early weeks were purgatory for Olivier, who was a terrible giggler when he joined the cast. Coward soon discovered this and, knowing that Olivier had already been sacked from one production for giggling, he told him frankly that unless he cured himself he'd be out on the street looking for another job before the year was out. Then he played on Olivier's weakness mercilessly, joking and fooling about on stage to make Olivier giggle, while remaining in complete control of himself.

For instance, he invented Roger, an imaginary dog with an unsavoury appetite for Olivier's private parts. He would conduct a whispered conversation with this unseen cur, while keeping a perfectly straight face. For Olivier, on tenterhooks to know what Roger would get up to next, it was torture.

Eventually the night came when a cure was effected and Olivier managed to beat Coward at his own game. He delivered his line, 'A friend of mine has a house on the edge of Cap Ferrat' according to the script, at which Coward ad-libbed, 'On the *edge?*' 'That's right,' came the confident reply, 'on the very edge' and for the first time he was able to look Coward right in the eye with complete confidence. He also got a jolly good laugh into the bargain. By the time they opened on Broadway his anxieties were over.

John Gielgud wasn't above the occasional slip in this respect, although his tendency to giggle never reached the proportions of Olivier's. Playing in *The Importance of Being Earnest* one hot afternoon to a very thin matinée audience, he let his concentration wander and he cast an eye over the house. There he noticed half a dozen old women in various parts of the stalls slumped so heavily asleep that they were hanging over the sides of their seats like empty glove puppets. The sight of them started him giggling over his tea. Anthony Ireland, who was on stage with him, picked up the vibes and soon the pair of them were hopelessly trying to force muffins down their throats in a attempt to regain their composure. It was a losing battle. By the end of the scene, the audience were also in hysterics at their efforts to keep themselves under control and the humour of the scene itself had been completely lost.

Coward's operetta *Conversation Piece* opened in February 1934 at His Majesty's Theatre, to be followed during the next two years by tours of his set of one-act plays *To-night at 8.30*, which he'd written for himself and Gertrude Lawrence.

Not long after the London opening of the latter Edward VIII sent a message that he'd like seats for the show – that very evening. Coward didn't receive this until late in the day. The house was booked out for weeks in advance and all he could do was ask friends whom he knew were booked in for that night whether they would mind giving up their tickets for the royal party. Generously they agreed and King Edward got his seats.

After the show he spent half an hour talking to Gertrude Lawrence in her dressing-room, but left the theatre without speaking to Coward and certainly without any word of thanks for the seats. So irritated was Coward by this apparent rudeness that he sent his own message to the Palace: 'Tell him that he may be King of England, but I'm King of the Theatre and I expect him to respect me as such.'

'Tell Noël Coward to go and .... himself,' came back the reply from the Palace.

Noël gave him ten out of ten for that.

After the Abdication, King Edward's brother, King George VI, and his Queen came to another Coward-Lawrence performance – with their own tickets. As they entered the Royal Box, the whole audience rose to greet them with tumultuous applause.

'What an entrance!' marvelled Gertrude Lawrence as she and Coward waited in the wings.

'What a part,' answered Coward.

He was still delighting New York audiences when *Tonight at 8.30* opened at the National Theatre. During the pre-Broadway run he'd scored a huge success in Washington DC with an impromptu addition brought about by a hiccup in the lighting box.

In *Ways and Means*, one of the nine sketches in the play, Gertrude Lawrence crossed the stage to switch out a light and the LX man missed his cue. The lamp flashed out before she reached it and then flashed on again.

Coward took a calm puff at his cigarette and remarked, 'The house is haunted', which may not be the funniest line he had invented, but was good enough to raise a merry laugh and save the scene.

Given his own sense of timing both in repartee and in his plays, it isn't surprising that Coward would become exasperated with other actors who spoilt the tempo of his lines. In the original production of *Present Laughter* he finally blew his top with an actress who was persistently slow with her lines. 'If you go on like this,' she shouted, immediately losing her temper, 'I'll throw something at you.'

'You might start with my cues,' snapped Coward.

He was gentler with actors he admired. Dame Sybil Thorndike invariably fluffed in the first act of *Waiting in the Wings*, Coward's play about elderly Thespians in a retirement home for old actresses, whenever he was out front. After that he dubbed her affectionately 'Fluffy Damsie'.

Lewis Casson played her aged beau in that production, dutifully arriving every week with flowers for his old love. Two years later, in the inaugural production of *Uncle Vanya* at the Chichester Festival Theatre, it was her turn to wag a gentle finger of admonition.

Dame Sybil was playing the nurse and Lewis Casson, Waffles. With the open stage at Chichester, there was no curtain to fall at the end of the scene in which Waffles has finished playing his guitar and has dropped off to sleep; the actors had to get up and walk off.

One night, as the scene came to an end, Dame Sybil got up to leave, but Lewis Casson, who was fairly elderly by this time, stayed slumbering in his chair.

'Waffles, Waffles,' the nurse called sweetly, but there wasn't a flicker of movement. 'Waffles, Waffles,' she called again, but louder. Still Lewis Casson sat slumped peacefully over his guitar. 'Waffles, Waffles,' she tried a third time, ever more anxious and strident. In the end she called sharply, 'Lewis!' at which he jumped to his feet and they made their exit.

Another great Dame of the theatre, Edith Evans, caused Noël Coward rather greater traumas than had Sybil Thorndike, when she was cast as Judith Bliss in the National Theatre's revival of *Hay Fever* in 1964, though Coward was the director on this occasion and not just a member of the audience.

His pleasure at being asked to direct one of his earliest creations was touching. He opened the first

TWO'S COMPANY; OR, AN EMBARRASSMENT
OF BLISSES.

Myra Arundel	. . . .	MISS HILDA MOORE.
David Bliss	. . . .	MR. W. GRAHAM BROWNE.
Mrs. Bliss	. . . .	MISS MARIE TEMPEST.

rehearsal with a little speech in which he told the cast, 'I'm thrilled and flattered and frankly a little flabbergasted that the National Theatre should have had the curious perceptiveness to choose a very early play of mine and to give it a cast that could play the Albanian telephone directory.' Then it was down to work.

It was soon obvious that director and leading lady had very different ways of approaching a new production. Where Coward expected his cast to be word perfect when they started rehearsing, Dame Edith insisted that the lines should come with the moves and a growing understanding of the part. It was all right for Noël Coward to bleat on about knowing the lines – he'd written them. She had to let them come naturally to make them sound natural. The problem was that in this case there was a certain amount of difficulty in them coming – one line in particular. Dame Edith would insist in upsetting Coward's carefully structured rhythm by saying, 'On a very clear day you can see Marlow,' instead of 'On a clear day you can see Marlow.'

After weeks of patient correction, Coward eventually stopped the scene and told her, 'Edith. The line is "On a clear day you can see Marlow." On a *very* clear day you can see Marlowe and Beaumont and Fletcher.'

Hay Fever went to Manchester for its try-out, to which Sir Laurence Olivier, then in charge of the National Theatre, was summoned by a distraught Coward, who told him that he'd have to sack Dame Edith Evans! After weeks of rehearsal she still hadn't come up to scratch.

This was something Sir Laurence was understandably loath to do and he said he would watch the show and speak to her afterwards. What he saw wasn't encouraging and it certainly wasn't Edith Evans. She didn't seem to know her lines, was unsure of where to go and what to do and in contrast to the other polished and highly promising performances looked quite at sea.

Round in the number-one dressing-room, Olivier was steeling himself to do the unthinkable deed of firing one of the country's leading actresses when he caught sight of a pair of unused false eyelashes lying among her make-up. He asked in astonishment why she hadn't worn them and both he and Coward were rendered almost speechless when Dame Edith replied, 'Well, dear, I didn't want to think of it as a performance.'

Sir Laurence left, having granted Dame Edith an unspoken reprieve, but the fun and games in Manchester weren't over. There was another sharp exchange with Coward after she completely lost her confidence one night and refused to go on. Heated words passed between them and the leading lady duly appeared in the wings to be led through that performance by the rest of the cast, who took it in turns to prompt her.

In one scene when almost everybody was on stage the whole thing ground to a terrible halt as Dame Edith missed a line that was to cue someone else's entrance. The prompter gave her the line three times from the wings, but as no one could indicate it was meant for her, Dame Edith occupied herself nervously with various bits of business, such as stroking a cushion, until she resolutely announced in the end, 'I won't say it. It's not my turn!'

However, these set-backs in Manchester were merely teething troubles, which are, after all, what a try-out is for. When the show came into London it received an enthusiastic response and turned out to be such a success that a wave of Coward revivals followed in its wake.

By now Noël Coward's acting had switched from the stage to lucrative guest appearances in films or television specials on both sides of the Atlantic. Like many of the critics of his plays, he realized that the theatre which had nourished him and in which his talent had blossomed had been replaced by a grainier and distinctly less attractive one, aptly summed up as 'kitchen-sink'.

Recognizing this, and smiling benignly at the status quo, he apologized for the filthy, scruffy clothes he was asked to wear as the landlord in Otto Preminger's film *Bunny Lake is Missing*, commenting, 'You'd really think I was a young modern actor on his way to rehearsal.'

Ways and means

THE MASTER'S CAREER as a director, and shortly after as a writer, followed close on the heels of his stage debut. Less than two months after his twelfth birthday he produced a matinée of *The Daisy Chain* at the Savoy Theatre, and a little later in the year he stage-managed a matinée of *The Prince's Bride* at the same theatre.

Throughout his teens plays and sketches from his own pen, and others written in collaboration with fellow actors, began to appear; some, like the *Rat Trap,* to be produced later once he'd made a name for himself.

As a playwright, his breakthrough came two months short of his twenty-first birthday. The play was inspired by an American impresario named Gilbert Miller, who had suggested that Coward should try writing a play for Sir Charles Hawtrey on an idea that Miller had come up with himself. He also had the title for the play: *I'll Leave It to You.*

Coward had a natural reluctance to write something based on someone else's ideas, but he set to, finished the piece, made a few changes recommended by Miller and waited for its try-out in Manchester.

In the end it wasn't thought strong enough to merit Hawtrey's attention, which more or less ruled out a London run. It was therefore left to Coward to find a producer and he had the good luck to interest Lady

33

Wyndham, who agreed to put it on at her New Theatre.

For a first production it was well received. 'Freshly written and brightly acted', was the verdict of the *Daily Mail*'s reviewer, who continued, 'the piece betrays a certain striving after ultra-comic effect. Mr Noël Coward, the author, who is not yet twenty-one, is almost too successful in making the younger nephew a most objectionable boy'.

I'll Leave It to You ran for four weeks in London and then slipped quietly away to join the growing pile of light comedies of the period. The next Coward play to be produced was 'a comedy of youth in three acts', which he called *The Young Idea* and which bore a considerable resemblance to Bernard Shaw's *You Never Can Tell,* which had inspired it.

When Coward had finished the manuscript he sent it to Shaw, who returned it a short while afterwards covered with carefully observed notes and accompanied by a long, detailed letter which told Coward that he had a promising future as a playwright, providing that he didn't read another word of Shaw's own work!

His prophecy proved true, though Shaw didn't always come to witness its fruits. Hearing that he was reluctant to see *Cavalcade,* which first appeared ten years after their correspondence over *The Young Idea,* Coward wrote to Shaw suggesting, 'As you've lived through the period, I'm sure you'll enjoy it.' Shaw thought otherwise, so Coward sent him a ticket for a box as his next attempt, along with a note saying, 'The box contains four seats – so you'll be able to bring *all* your friends.'

(This recalls a similar exchange between Shaw and Churchill over one of the former's new productions.

Shaw sent Churchill a couple of tickets for the opening night with the note, 'Bring a friend, if you have one.' These were returned by Churchill saying that he wasn't free that evening but would like a couple of tickets 'for the second night, if you have one.')

Noël Coward's correspondence often sparkled with the same sense of mocking fun that enlivened his dialogue. In the early years of his career he obtained much innocent amusement from signing his letters with a succession of famous (and not so famous) names: Harriet Beecher Stowe, Arnold Bennett, Benjamin Disraeli and, on at least one occasion, that hitherto unknown 'celebrity' Cordelia Rhubarb.

He played other games too. The novelist G.B. Stern once received a letter from Coward written in the manner of village tittle-tattle and ending with the comment, 'and isn't it too dreadful about poor Rebecca West?'

This reminded Miss Stern that she hadn't actually heard from Rebecca West for several weeks and prompted her to send telegrams to the authoress, the authoress's sister and Coward, asking what terrible fate had befallen her friend.

The following morning she received four telegrams by return. The first, from Rebecca West's sister, expressed surprise, but reassurance that nothing was wrong. The other three read:

ISN'T IT TOO DREADFUL ABOUT GEOFFREY MOSS?

MAY SINCLAIR

ISN'T IT TOO FRIGHTFUL ABOUT BERTA RUCK?

ROSE MACAULAY

ISN'T IT TOO TERRIBLY SAD ABOUT NOËL COWARD?

E.M. DELL

In New York once he tried to send a friend an opening night telegram from the Western Union office on Broadway. Fiorello La Guardia was mayor at the time and, for fun, Coward signed his name at the bottom.

'You can't sign Mayor La Guardia's name to this,' the clerk told Coward.

'Why not?'

'Because you aren't Mayor La Guardia.'

So Coward crossed out his name and wrote 'Noël Coward' in its place.

'And you can't sign it Noël Coward, either!' the clerk told him.

'But I *am* Noël Coward.'

'Well, in that case you can sign it Mayor La Guardia,' said the clerk.

Among the gifts of his imagination was a wonderful felicity for names which perfectly mirrored his subtle use of words in general. His inventions appeared effortless and endless. When a brash but brainless lady journalist interviewing him in Switzerland asked him about his neighbours, Coward replied politely that he enjoyed the company of friends like Joan Sutherland and the Nivens, and added pleasantly, 'I'm seeing Yehudi this very afternoon.'

'Yehudi who?'

'Yehudi Bankhead.'

Fools weren't suffered lightly, as I once discovered to my cost when he came to see me in *Relatively Speaking,* Alan Ayckbourn's very first West End hit, which also had Celia Johnson and Michael Hordern in the cast. In order to jolly up my rather shabby and bare dressing-room, I put up one of those large and rather garish posters of a Spanish bull on the inside of my door. One night Noël came round with his friend Graham Payn, the actor, to see me. I always felt rather nervous in the Master's presence, because in his later years he could be quite irascible. We were talking fairly easily when there was suddenly one of those awful pauses when you feel you have to say something. In desperation I pointed to the poster and said, 'I got that in Spain.' To which he immediately replied, 'I didn't think you got it in Aberdeen.'

I got off fairly lightly that time compared with the photographer who pointed his camera at Coward at the press reception following his show *Pacific 1860* and asked, 'Could you tell me your name, please?'

'I recommend you to *Who's Who* – and hell,' replied the author.

Nor did he have much time for pomposity. In answer to a letter from one of America's corporate magnates which began, 'From the desk of . . .', Coward replied, 'Dear Desk of . . .'.

False modesty didn't cut much ice either. After Lawrence of Arabia slid into obscurity in the RAF, Coward began a letter to him with, 'Dear 338171, or may I call you 338 . . .?' (According to a recent correspondent in *The Times,* 'Coward apparently didn't know that in the RAF the first shall be last; he should have written, "may I call you 171 . . .?"')

A final word on Coward's way with names. He developed a fail-safe method of getting the better of people whom he'd met and whose names he'd either forgotten or never known.

'How do you manage?' he used to be asked. 'You

must meet dozens of people who expect you to know their names, when of course you don't.'

Coward would reply, 'I always say to them "What is your name?" and they say "Frank", or whatever it is, and then I say, "I know your first name is Frank as well as I know my own is Noël; I mean what is your second name?" Whereas if they say "Jones" I say, "Well, I know you're Jones as well as I know I'm Coward, I mean what is your first name?"'

After that, he went on to explain, 'I always add, "And how is Muriel?" which puts them at a complete loss, because they have to think, "Do I know Muriel?"'

But back to Coward the writer and director, whose first major triumph in *The Vortex* came only a couple of years after *The Young Idea.* Its opening in Hampstead was undertaken on a pretty thin shoe-string. Gladys Calthrop, whom he'd asked to design the scenery, and who worked closely with Coward in the years to come, was given £25 to cover all her expenses and was told she couldn't have any more because there wasn't any more!

The following year, 1925, saw the first production of *Hay Fever,* which owed a great deal in its conception to Coward's first Broadway visit, when he lived in New York for six months with practically no money. There he met Laurette Taylor, the Irish actress who had achieved a huge success in London just before the First World War in her husband's play *Peg o' My Heart.*

She lived in some style on Riverside Drive, to where she was in the habit of inviting a few actor friends on Sunday evenings. Her two children also liked to invite friends of theirs, who usually had no knowledge of the theatre and were altogether rather intimidated by the arty conversation and stage jargon.

Coward's imagination was evidently caught by Laurette Taylor's word games, which she would announce with relish during the course of these evenings. To their dismay and acute embarrassment guests had to take it in turns to 'do something in the manner of the word'. Invariably they wouldn't do it to her satisfaction and she would tell them so: 'No, no, no! That's not the way to do it at all.' After which she would do whatever had been asked – flawlessly!

Her family applauded enthusiastically and the guests withdrew even deeper into their shells. In the end the evenings became such a source of terror in New York that few invitations were accepted to Laurette Taylor's Sunday evening get-togethers.

This was marvellous material for Noël Coward, of course, and, substituting Judith Bliss for Laurette

Hay Fever, November 1964
Edith Evans and Maggie Smith

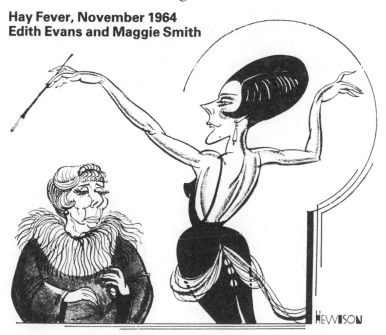

Taylor and her children, Simon and Sorel, for Miss Taylor's offspring, he constructed the justly famous 'game' scene from the second act of *Hay Fever* and built up one of his most enduring and popular comedies – written in three days!

With Marie Tempest playing Judith Bliss, in what many considered her finest performance, *Hay Fever* had a highly profitable West End run – and it was in good company. For a week in July 1925 Coward had no fewer than three of his 'straight' plays running in London: *The Vortex* and *Fallen Angels* as well as *Hay Fever* – not to mention the revue *On With the Dance,* of which he was part author and composer.

While the majority of critics spared little with their praise, James Agate's was a lone voice cutting against the general tide of adulation:

> Mr Coward is credited with the capacity to turn out these very highly polished pieces of writing in an incredibly short time. And if rumour and the illustrated weeklies are to be believed, he writes his plays in a flowered dressing-gown before breakfast. But what I want to know is what kind of work he intends to do after breakfast, when he is clothed in his right mind.

Lilian Braithwaite, who was playing opposite Coward in *The Vortex* at the time, was able to get the better of Agate in an exchange they had some years later at a theatrical reception. 'My dear Lilian, I have long wanted to tell you that in my opinion you are the second best actress in London,' said the then critic of the *Sunday Times*.

'Thank you so much,' replied Miss Braithwaite. 'I

shall cherish that – coming from the second best dramatic critic.'

The successes of 1925 were followed by a fallow period for Noël Coward as a playwright on the London stage. In 1926 *This Was a Man* was produced on Broadway and on the continent, but never found its way into an English theatre. Then there were the disappointments a year later when *Home Chat* and *Sirocco* both failed. 1928 saw the success of his revue *This Year of Grace*. But it wasn't until 1929 that he returned to the West End with a smash hit of a play, and a musical one at that – *Bitter Sweet*.

This 'operette' had been written for the impresario C.B. Cochran and in its production bore a small but significant stamp of his particular feeling for the theatre.

In the published version of the play Coward followed the standard convention of musical plays and took the chorus off the stage whenever he wanted important dialogue to take place between the principals. But in the scene in the café in Vienna (the second scene in Act II) they had to keep nipping off to the bar and then fortuitously reappearing, having finished their drinks just as the principals came to the end of their conversation.

Cochran thought this was a weakness compared with the carefully structured realism of the other scenes. Coward took his advice and completely rewrote the second act, so that all the important dialogue could be incorporated into the first scene, leaving the café scene a bustling hubbub, with the whole company on stage and hardly any dialogue until the music suddenly stopped and the violent quarrel leading to the fatal duel flared up. Dramatically, this heightened the tension enormously.

It was in gratitude for guidance and support like this that Coward dedicated *Bitter Sweet* to Cochran with the lines,

My help for ages past,
My hope for years to come.

The production wouldn't have been complete without a *mot* from the Master and the one that stuck was delivered when word reached Coward of the accident that had befallen the diminutive Ivy St Helier, for whom Coward had written the part of Manon la Crevette.

'Have you heard?' a flustered actor asked Coward one day. 'Ivy's broken her leg in two places.'

'I didn't know there *were* two places,' replied Coward.

Bitter Sweet collected some impressive statistics in its run, which spanned the best part of two years. Approaching a million people paid to see it in London and it took £385,000 at the box office. It also spawned twelve marriages and eight children among the members of the company; it wasn't just the audience who recognized this as Coward's most unashamedly romantic musical comedy.

American audiences fell for it with the same enthusiasm, and *Bitter Sweet* brought Coward another memorable Broadway triumph.

He took a holiday which started with a ten-day visit to Hollywood and then moved across the Pacific for six months. In Shanghai Coward went down with flu. While he was recovering from this in bed, with nothing else to do, he remembered a promise he had made to Gertrude Lawrence that he would write a play for the two of them. Four days later he put the final full stop to *Private Lives* and subsequently hardly altered a word of that original draft.

Gertrude Lawrence was in New York when the script arrived. She read it and, with uncharacteristic frugality, dashed off a terse cable in reply: 'Play delightful. Nothing wrong that can't be fixed.' For once economy had not been the wisest choice.

Only recently risen from his sick bed, Coward was incensed when he read the message and sent off a series of tart replies to the effect that the only thing that might require fixing was Miss Lawrence's performance.

All she had been trying to say, however, was that she was contracted to André Charlot for the proposed dates but was sure that something could be arranged to accommodate all parties. In the event, Coward took some convincing.

For any actor, following Noël Coward and Gertie Lawrence in *Private Lives* is a challenge, but to be directed by Coward in the play leaves very little room for cover. Googie Withers, who took over from Kay Hammond as Amanda in the 1946 revival, knew about this. She recalls feeling reasonably pleased with her performance in acts two and three. It was in the first act that something didn't quite jell. She asked Coward, as director, what was wrong.

'Too piss-elegant. Too piss-elegant,' was his reply.

He summed up my performance as Roland Maule in Nigel Patrick's production of *Present Laughter* at the Queen's Theatre with the same succinctness. Nigel was playing Noël's part of Garry Essendine in this revival as well as directing it and right at the end of rehearsals he

DRESSING-DOWNS AND DRESSING GOWNS

Joanna Lyppiatt	MISS JUDY CAMPBELL
Liz Essendine	MISS JOYCE CAREY
Roland Maule	MR. JAMES DONALD
Garry Essendine	MR. NOEL COWARD

politely and tactfully asked Noël if he would like to
come and see a final run through to evaluate the
qualities of the production. I'd never met him before
and I was horrified when he accepted Nigel's
invitation. To add to my discomfort, he watched the
run-through from an elegant chair positioned at the
edge of the stage, sitting only a few feet away from the
company.

My part, as the fanatical playwright who tries to
persuade Essendine that he's wasting his talent on
West End trash and should really act in his own ex-

perimental plays, is a highly emotional one. As may be
imagined, I played it with added vehemence in that
particular run-through.

When we had finished he worked his way through
the cast, making various criticisms. At last the pale
blue eyes settled on me. There was a pause and I gave a
rather sickly smile. 'You frighten me to death,' said
Coward – and that was all.

From directing a cast of five in the original production
of *Private Lives,* Coward turned his attention to
something of an altogether different dimension and
presented Cochran with one of the most ambitious and
colossal productions of his and certainly of Noël
Coward's career – *Cavalcade.*

By his own admission, Coward felt the 'urge to test
my producing powers on a large scale' and the chance
discovery of a back copy of the *Illustrated London News*
with a picture of a troopship leaving for the Boer War
gave him the idea he was looking for. It might equally
well have been the French Revolution, or the storming
of the Winter Palace at St Petersburg – though the
latter might not have been quite so warmly welcomed
by a people which had seen the collapse of the
first-ever Labour Government in the summer and were
to see a 'National' Government returned in the autumn
with a poll of 558 seats to the Opposition's 56!

Cochran arranged to provide Coward with Drury
Lane for a September opening which left him a bare
four months to write, plan, cast, and rehearse the
mammoth production.

With Gladys Calthrop as designer, he buried himself
away in Goldenhurst, his farmhouse in Kent, to put
together the show during the early summer. Among

other technical details it called for was the installation
of a number of hydraulic lifts in the Drury Lane stage.

When it came to composing the music of the
'Mirabelle' waltz, which Coward introduced to typify
the Gaiety show of 1900, he bought up fifty
pounds-worth of Victorian and Edwardian scores,
went home in a taxi with these piled in beside him and
absorbed the whole lot before sitting down to compose
his own score, which was perfectly in keeping with the
period.

With a time span stretching over thirty years
Coward needed a large cast, and if it had no other
merit *Cavalcade* provided much needed employment for
many old actors and actresses in small parts. There
were getting on for a hundred of these and from the
front of the dress circle where he sat to direct Coward
didn't have a chance of recognizing each of them, even
if he'd been able to put a name to the face. To get over
this, he had each of them wear numbers on their backs
like members of a rugger team. Directing by numbers
in this way, he had only to consult a master list to
identify everyone on stage and give personal directions
to each of them by name, which boosted morale no
end.

Because of its vast technical complexities it was
impossible to break in *Cavalcade* gently out of town and
four full dress rehearsals were called as a substitute.
During the last of these one of the hydraulic lifts
jammed, making it impossible for the stage crew of
almost a hundred to change scenes.

As the electricians and engineers sweated and
struggled to rectify the fault Gladys Calthrop and
Coward pondered the matter on stage, wondering, like
everyone else, what would happen if the same problem

arose on the opening night.

Coward stood there, deep in thought, carefully and methodically picking his nose. Beside him was his unflappable stage manager, Danny O'Neill, who watched the Master with close interest before suddenly saying to him, 'Wave when you come to the bridge!'

There couldn't have been a better way of breaking the rising tension, and as everyone roared with laughter, the lifts came to life once more and the dress rehearsal resumed after a two-hour break.

After the heady success of the *Cavalcade* opening Coward set off on his travels once more to recover from the exertions of such a mammoth undertaking. However, his pen wasn't idle. On his return he presented Cochran with a crisp new revue, appropriately entitled *Words and Music.*

For that brilliant couple Alfred Lunt and Lynn Fontanne he wrote *Design for Living* and this occupied him on Broadway for the early part of 1933. He then returned to London to direct a revival of *Hay Fever* at the Shaftesbury Theatre, again under the patronage of C.B. Cochran.

Their next and, as it turned out, last collaboration came with *Conversation Piece,* a sentimental Regency comedy that Coward had conceived primarily as a vehicle for the enchanting French actress Yvonne Printemps. The male lead had been offered to the American actor Romney Brent. He wasn't so sure about the part and after reading the script told Coward, 'I'm a comedian – I can't play a distinguished romantic aristocrat of middle age.' Coward convinced him otherwise and Brent later admitted to Cochran, 'I am an actor and therefore susceptible to flattery, so I fell.'

They both realized the error of this less than a week before the opening, when Coward had to tell Romney Brent that he wasn't going to let him open. For his part, Brent was hugely relieved and more than happy to go along with Coward's decision to take over the part himself – on the condition 'that I come to every rehearsal and watch you struggle with that awful part'.

If Coward did struggle, it wasn't obvious to the opening night audience, who were charmed by Mlle Printemps, beguiled by Gladys Calthrop's lavish sets and glorious Regency costumes and totally captivated by the haunting melodies that were established as a Noël Coward hallmark. In this case the tune on everyone's lips as they left that night was the romantic theme-song sung by Yvonne Printemps, 'I'll Follow My Secret Heart'.

Cochran had followed the charming gesture of giving Coward a small present on each opening night and after rummaging through antique shops for something suitable for *Conversation Piece,* he settled on a Regency snuff-box that might double as a cigarette case. This he presented to his collaborator of nine years with the prescient inscription 'In memory of a not altogether unsuccessful association.'

Conversation Piece was a fortnight into its run when Cochran dropped into His Majesty's to have a chat with Coward in his dressing-room. He found him strangely ill at ease and after a few uncomfortable minutes Coward asked, 'Did you get my long letter? I wanted you to get it before you saw me.'

Cochran hadn't received anything from him and at Coward's urging made enquiries at home to see whether or not it had been delivered. There he discovered that Blake, his miniature dachshund, had

taken a liking to opening the mail and had set to with
Coward's letter while his master was opening the rest
of his breakfast post.

From the portion that had survived Blake's attention, Cochran gathered that Coward had decided the
time had come to present his own and other people's
plays himself, in partnership with other colleagues –
notably Jack Wilson, his business manager and close
associate for many years.

Cochran's own premonition had proved accurate
and after presenting Coward with the unmistakable
evidence that Blake really had been the cause of his
delay in responding to it, the two men made their
professional parting on the best of terms.

Years later, *Conversation Piece* was the focal point for
a memorable exchange between its author and another
great name in the British theatre, Richard Burton. He
had just scored his first success as a young actor and,
during a spell in New York, had a call from Coward
asking him if he could do a day's work on a recording
of *Conversation Piece* that he was making.

Burton told Coward he'd be delighted and a short
time afterwards an agent called him with the details of
the contract and the fee – $200. The young actor told
him more or less what to do with his fee and refused
point blank to spend a day working for such a paltry
sum.

Ten minutes later the telephone rang again and
Coward's perfectly enunciated tones came down the
line: 'You will do *Conversation Piece* for $200 – and you
will like it.'

The rising star humbly did as he was told.

In the spring of 1934 Coward put on his director's
hat once more and brought S.N. Behrman's *Biography*

to the West End, starring the American actress Ina Claire. This was his first production with Jack Wilson away from Cochran's protection, and the Master was obviously out to impress.

In the end he rather missed the boat. Laurence Olivier, cast by Coward to play opposite Miss Claire, had misgivings towards the end of rehearsals about Coward's obsession with pace.

As a result of working on *Private Lives* he appreciated the store Coward set by finding the right (usually fast) rhythm, but where *Private Lives* was a vigorous allegro, *Biography* was written to a gentle andante. Quickening the pace didn't improve the piece and Miss Claire, who could rival Gertie Lawrence with the tempo of her playing was almost rushed off her feet by the hectic demands made upon her by Coward.

For once his zeal backfired. His London audiences were bemused by the production and after a helter skelter run of four or five weeks it closed.

. If his theatrical instinct hadn't quite hit the mark with *Biography* it still hadn't lost any of its edge when, a few years later, it helped him through a tricky moment in rehearsals for *Operette.* The year was 1938 and for a brief moment the rising international tension had switched its sights from Nazi Germany to the imminent birth of a baby to Princess Juliana of the Netherlands.

For the cast of *Operette,* tension was mounting as they struggled to master a particularly difficult 'silence' scene. Everyone was becoming edgy, hampering progress even more, when the air was suddenly rent by the piercing scream of a klaxon horn.

'Juliana's baby! Thank God!' said Coward crisply, helping the scene to change gear and move smoothly to its conclusion.

When Adolf Hitler moved to the centre of the international stage, Noël Coward was called upon to serve his country in a variety of ways.

During the phoney war he found himself ensconced in a comfortable apartment above the Place Vendôme in Paris, where he occupied himself with turgid missives from Whitehall that came under the vague heading of propaganda. This was not wholly to his liking and he soon made himself unpopular with the mandarins by sending a succession of tart reports and enquiries. Among these was his comment on a proposed RAF propaganda drop ordered by Chamberlain and Lord Halifax, his foreign secretary – men for whom Coward had little regard as being the architects of appeasement. Invited to comment on the contents of the message they intended distributing over enemy territory, Coward replied, 'If the policy of His Majesty's Government is to bore the Germans to death, I don't think we have the time.'

Once he was allowed to turn his hand to 'propaganda' that he understood and respected, the results were truly masterful and when his film about the Royal Navy, *In Which We Serve,* went on general release it was acclaimed as being the finest account of active service produced during the hostilities.

This was due in no small measure to Coward's painstaking attention to detail. As the scriptwriter, star and producer, he worked closely with his director, David Lean, to create a film that did full justice to the sufferings of the Senior Service, which were not always fully appreciated on the Home Front.

In this they were given invaluable help by his friend Lord Louis Mountbatten, whose own experiences as commander of HMS *Kelly* had been Coward's inspiration. Thanks to him, Coward was able to include

authentic elements of life on board a warship and to
pull important strings in the Admiralty. At one time
they needed a genuine ship's company for the filming,
complete with the clothes they wore when at sea! At a
time of war, with the navy stretched to its limits, this
wasn't easy to come by, but Mountbatten persuaded
the Second Sea Lord, who was in charge of Naval
Personnel, to release all hands of a ship in dock under
repair for a week's filming.

As a gesture of thanks Coward invited the Second
Sea Lord to attend the filming, with which he was
greatly impressed – so much so that he asked if he
could see some of the rushes. Coward was more' than
happy to oblige and he was shown a scene in which
one of the seamen, played by John Mills, had to tell a
Chief Petty Officer (Bernard Miles), that he'd heard
from home that the Chief's wife had been killed in an
air-raid. It is one of the most moving scenes in the film
and the Admiral was deeply affected.

'By jove, Coward,' he said when the screening was
over, 'that convinces me you were right to ask for a
proper ship's company, *real* sailors. No actors could
possibly have done that.'

Perhaps it was just as well he didn't catch sight of
the harmonica player who appeared on the set to work
on the soundtrack. His playing was not of the first
order, as a very few bars confirmed. Coward gazed at
him with disdain and commented, 'Look at him – the
eager look of the inefficient.'

If that sounds a bit harsh, especially in wartime, it is
only because Coward set himself such high standards
of attainment and then expected everyone else to rise
to meet them.

Acting Sub-Lieutenant Laurence Olivier's spell in

naval uniform came in for rather sterner scrutiny from his superiors than had Coward's endeavours with *In Which We Serve*. On his first day as a pilot at the Fleet Air Arm base at Worthy Down, an unfortunate piece of taxiing left his own plane wrecked and two others damaged. There was uncertainty about him off duty as well. Whatever the Senior Service may have thought of Coward's portrayal of the destroyer's skipper in his film, at least two seasoned officers were sceptical about Olivier portraying another naval hero. Soon after his entry to the Ward Room at Worthy Down, a couple of old Commanders, regulars in the service, eyed the newcomer suspiciously and aired their views with awful clarity.

'New fellow over there, know how he is?' asked the first.

'Yes,' replied his colleague. 'Another actor fellow – name's Olivier.'

'Oh! Heard he played Nelson in a Hollywood film not so long ago.'

'Quite so.'

'Ridiculous! The chap doesn't look a damn bit like Nelson.'

A graphic example of Coward's marvellously delicate appreciation of stage craft came in the run of his 1951 comedy *Relative Values,* which he directed, with Gladys Cooper as the Countess of Marshwood and Angela Baddeley as the housemaid Moxie (Mrs Moxton). Some time into the run Gladys commented that Angela was regularly losing a couple of fairly easy laughs in a scene they played together. Coward decided to watch the next night to see if anything was noticeably wrong, but nothing struck him as being obviously out of place; it was just that two of his funniest lines passed without a

flicker of amusement from the house. The next night
the situation was just the same, but it took an eye as
finely focused as Coward's to discover what was amiss.

The only detail that had altered from his rehearsals
was Gladys Cooper's sitting position in a wing chair. In
the course of the run she had settled back into it – by
nothing more than a few inches, but even this tiny
amount had altered the scene drastically. In order to
look directly into the Countess's eyes, Angela Baddeley
had had to turn her head upstage by a fraction of an
inch.

Coward noted this and suggested to Gladys that she
should try sitting a little further forward, as she had
been at the start. When she did this, without a word
being spoken to Angela Baddeley the laughs started to
return and were soon even bigger than they had been
at the outset.

There were similar problems with *After the Ball,*
which Robert Helpmann directed for Coward in 1954.
This was a musical based on Oscar Wilde's play *Lady
Windermere's Fan*, which presented Helpmann with the
awkward tensions of two masters of comedy working
in different directions.

To add to his problems there was one impossibly
difficult number which he wanted cut from the show,
to be replaced by a comedy scene. However, the
actress scripted to sing the number held on to it like
grim death and became so nervous when it was finally
axed that on the opening night she missed every laugh
in the comedy scene, one after the other, like a tennis
player swatting at the ball with a stringless racket.

Coward and Helpmann watched together in horror
from their box until Coward finally left his seat and set
off for the wings. 'I'm the director, Noël,' Helpmann,

hurrying after, reminded him, 'and you're not to speak
to anyone until after the show.' As an afterthought he
added, 'It's very difficult to get a laugh when you're
nervous.'

'She couldn't get a laugh if she pulled a kipper out
of her ....' snapped Coward, which only resulted in
them both lapsing into hysterics.

When they reached the wings the unfortunate
actress was offstage and the laughs were drifting back
from the house. 'She's pulled it out,' quipped Coward.
But the situation deteriorated as the run progressed,
leading Coward to further sour comments such as,
'Trouble with her, she was dropped on her head when
she was forty.'

There were other private feuds lurking backstage
among the cast of *After the Ball,* which starred Vanessa
Lee. Irene Browne, playing the Duchess of Berwick,
began to take grave exception to the uninhibited
success which greeted the delightful juvenile girl,
Patricia Cree, whose performance as the Duchess's
youngest daughter, Lady Agatha Carlisle, won glowing
notices in every town in which they played. Her
resentment built up and found an opportunity for
expression only in Bristol, where Miss Cree was late
for an entrance. The two ladies left the stage together
at the end of the scene in question but no sooner were
they in the wings than Miss Browne turned on her
victim.

'Oh, don't hit her, Irene', intervened Vanessa Lee.
'Poor little thing – she's as thin as a match!'

'Exactly,' retorted Miss Browne, 'she should be
struck and thrown away.'

The mid-1950s saw a number of television productions of Coward's work, not all of them wholly to his

J.H.DOWD

[Blithe Spirit

M.O.I.

Mme. Arcati . . . . MARGARET RUTHERFORD

liking. In 1956 CBS persuaded him to direct *Blithe Spirit,* with Claudette Colbert, who became the butt of one of Coward's most celebrated retorts when she apologized at rehearsal one day, 'I'm sorry, I knew these lines backwards last night,' only to be told by Noël, 'And that's exactly the way you're saying them this morning.'

Five years later, the rehearsals for *Sail Away* offered equally entertaining exchanges with Elaine Stritch.

Among the wonderfully witty songs Coward had written for this vivacious American star was one based on the sort of daft sayings you find in phrase books. This had the first line, 'When the Tower of Babel fell ...' which Miss Stritch sang for the first time in rehearsal with the pronunciation 'Babble'.

'It's *bayble,* Stritchie,' called Noël from the stalls.

'It's what?'

'*Bayble.* It rhymes with table.'

However, she resolutely insisted on pronouncing the word 'babble', as she had always done. It meant a sort of mixed-up language, didn't it? And she had never heard anyone pronounce it the way Coward did.

'Babble,' she maintained staunchly.

'That's a fabble,' he answered.

Earlier in the proceedings Coward had faced difficulties with other members of the cast – dogs. Elaine Stritch needed a dozen to walk on the end of a lead when she appeared on board ship and the trainer who paraded the dogs before Coward for the 'audition' in the Savoy Theatre brought along a whole circus act of four-footed gymnasts and acrobats which went through their party pieces while Coward sat impassively in the stalls.

When there was a break in the proceedings, he pointed to a small dog sitting quietly by the side of the stage, minding its own business, and asked, 'What's that dog's name?'

'That's Suzie, Mr Coward,' replied the trainer. 'She'll be on in a minute and once she's under those lights you'll really see something.'

'Any animal that's smart enough *not* to want to go into the theatre is smart enough to play the lead,' commented Coward and cast Suzie immediately.

If dogs were one problem with *Sail Away,* that other half of the stage bugbear, children, were another. There was one child in particular, a bewitching little girl who appeared in the nursery scene with Elaine Stritch, who seemed quite capable of completely stealing it from the star.

In the interests of ensuring that the audience kept their eyes on Miss Stritch, it was suggested to Coward that the little girl should be dropped. He had other ideas and, turning disadvantage to advantage, had the brainwave of getting the child to smoke during the scene, so that Miss Stritch could catch sight of her early on in her song, and move to take away the cigarette, which would force the child to run off in order to finish it.

The upshot of this was that he gave the audience a brief glimpse of the child and then got rid of her to let them concentrate on the star, while getting a big laugh into the bargain.

Would that all directing were that easy. Unfortunately the new generation of actors that crossed Coward's path, especially those of the method school, did not find favour with the Master. Expressing his general exasperation with the tedious earnestness he felt was enveloping the stage, he told one of these disciples who was constantly stopping rehearsals with enquiries about the motivation for his part, 'Your motivation is your pay packet on Friday. Now get on with it.'

On with the dance

AT THE TURN of the 1920s André Charlot's was the leading name in the world of 'intimate revue' and it was inevitable that the ambitious Coward would strive to make his acquaintance. Beatrice Lillie, herself established as one of the brightest lights in Charlot's shows, made the introduction.

Charlot listened impassively while Coward sang several songs with youthful exuberance before taking aside their mutual friend to tell her, 'Bea, never do that to me again. That boy has no talent whatsoever!'

He was to change his mind later.

Meanwhile Beatrice Lillie continued to take the world, both on and off the stage, by storm. In 1920 she married Sir Robert Peel and so acquired the title which allowed her her time-honoured quips, such as the response to telephone callers that she enjoyed using for a while, 'C'est Lady Peel qui parle.' Her long friendship with Coward stemmed from the happy meeting of two highly creative and wickedly impish minds. In quick-fire repartee few could match her but, like Coward's, her remarks were invariably balanced by an awareness of the occasion.

Dining at Buckingham Palace once, wearing a recently acquired and outrageously expensive evening gown, she fell victim to a hapless waiter who managed to tip a soup plate and its entire contents into her lap.

A terrible pause settled on the conversation. The poor waiter looked fit to die of embarrassment until Miss Lillie spared him further tribulation by declaiming in mock annoyance, 'Never darken my Dior again.'

Under different circumstances her answers were less modulated. Seated at another dinner party, this time adorned with the celebrated Peel pearls, she attracted the envious gaze of a fellow diner of slight acquaintance, who reached for the string of exquisite gems, bit one to test its authenticity and then announced in triumph, 'They're not real. They're cultured.'

'And how would you know,' answered their owner, 'with false teeth?'

Then there was the occasion in Chicago when she was having her hair done in the city's smartest salon as one of its other celebrity clients breezed in. Looking round disdainfully, Mrs Armour, wife of one of the city's principal meat packing millionaires, told her crimper, 'I'd have arranged to come at another time if I'd known there were going to be theatricals here.'

Her remark went unanswered for a couple of minutes until Beatrice Lillie was ready to leave, at which point she told the proprietor in penetrating tones, 'You may tell the butcher's wife that Lady Peel has finished now.'

Like Noël Coward, Beatrice Lillie had an inspired knack of generating humour from slightly adjusting the meaning of what had been said. Once, on a Broadway stage, she and a fellow leading lady were confronted by a stills photographer at the end of rehearsals who asked, 'Could you step back a little further, ladies?'

'Why?' snapped Miss Lillie, who wanted to get away.

'Because he wants to focus,' explained her co-star.

'What – both of us?' retorted Miss Lillie.

Like Coward, too, Beatrice Lillie didn't always have things her own way in the matter of repartee.

When she first appeared with Jack Buchanan, who was making his London debut in the show *A to Z*, she was on the receiving end – thanks mainly to the innocence of her youth.

At that time Bea was being cast in 'trouser' parts, and had become so proficient as a stage transvestite that she was known as the best dressed man in London.

In spite of this, theatrical propriety still required her to dress with the other girls in the cast and in the Prince of Wales Theatre, where they were playing, the men dressed on one side of the stage, the girls on the other.

Her constant appearance in a range of male attire never failed to amuse Jack Buchanan, whose own elegant figure in evening clothes was soon to make him a world-wide screen idol. 'Tell me, Beattie,' he asked her one day, 'which way do you dress – left or right?' As an actress who had only recently learned that flies had something to do with what lay above the stage, his question left her completely baffled. He tried again. 'Come on, Beattie. There's no need to be shy. Which side do you dress on?' Eventually the penny dropped. 'Oh, I see,' she answered. 'In Number Five. Stage left.' Jack Buchanan loved that.

It wasn't long before Coward was among them to join in the fun. In spite of his first disappointing encounter with André Charlot he was able to persuade Lord Lathom, a friend who had been one of the backers of *A to Z*, to support a revue of his own.

Lathom liked Coward, liked his work and arranged for Charlot to join them in Switzerland, where he was recovering from tuberculosis, to look through what Coward had written and hear the music and lyrics he had composed.

Although his attitude towards Coward warmed considerably, Charlot wasn't convinced that the material was strong enough to sustain a full revue, particularly one that would be carrying top-of-the-bill names. Consequently, he suggested that Coward work with a couple of collaborators: Ronald Jeans on the book and Philip Braham on the score. This was the trio that created *London Calling!*, the show that gave Noël Coward his name in lights for the first time.

Among his contributions to the show was what *The Times* critic described as 'a broad and amusing satire on very modern poetry', which Coward had entitled *The Swiss Family Whittlebot*. This was a fairly blatant parody of the Sitwells' verse which contained lines such as:

Beloved, it is dawn, I rise
To smell the roses sweet,
Emphatic are my hips and thighs,
Phlegmatic are my feet.

Everyone but the Sitwells thought it was a scream. However, Osbert Sitwell took the matter very much to heart and wrote to Coward in terms of such acrimony that for a while Coward thought it was all a huge joke. Further tart correspondence showed that it was anything but a joke and for several years they pursued a dogged feud by mail and cut each other ostentatiously whenever they met in public.

It took a meeting in New York several years after

London Calling! to clear the air, after which Osbert persuaded his sister Edith to cable Coward her words of forgiveness. After that they all rubbed along quite cheerfully together.

London Calling! also featured some nifty footwork on the part of Coward, who had sweated under the taxing tuition of his American choreographer – a young man who went by the name of Fred Astaire.

In 1924 André Charlot produced one of his most spectacular revues of all, culling items from previous successes. After a try-out at the Golders Green Hippodrome it crossed the Atlantic to open on Broadway in the New Year. Heading the cast were Beatrice Lillie, Gertrude Lawrence and Jack Buchanan and the New York notices were ecstatic, with headlines such as 'LONDON STARS TRIUMPHANT. NEW YORK SURRENDERS TO CHARLOT REVUE GIRLS.' A newspaper boy started singing a rhyme of his own one evening and soon all over town you could hear people humming:

> Lillie and Lawrence,
> Lawrence and Lillie,
> If you haven't seen them,
> You're perfectly silly.

The same three stars took another of Charlot's revues to the States the following year and after six months on Broadway undertook a short tour before playing in Hollywood for three weeks, during which the town was at their feet.

On the last night they saw all the Hollywood male stars in the stalls gradually leaving their seats before the finale. This was a little unsettling, but they battled on towards the end, putting a brave face on disappointment.

Jack Buchanan appeared in his full Highland costume to sing the opening bars of the last song. Gertrude Lawrence followed dressed as Flora Macdonald; then came Beatrice Lillie as Bonnie Prince Charlie. Individually they scanned the house and realized that there wasn't a single one of the male stars left in their seats.

Midway through the song all was explained as they suddenly started trooping on from the wings one by one, their trousers rolled up to their knees.

Rudolf Valentino was sporting a Highland headdress which he had borrowed from one of the girls in the chorus. Charlie Chaplin had tied his tails round his waist like a kilt. The Marx brothers had kitted themselves out with red beards. Richard Barthlemas was wearing a tam o'shanter, and, for a reason known only to him, Jack Gilbert came on carrying a ladder.

The invaders completely took over the finale. They made speeches and Chaplin, who was then refusing to make 'talkies', delivered his in mime. It was a night few of the audience or cast were ever likely to forget!

Some years later Jack Buchanan appeared in his musical *Stand Up and Sing* at the London Hippodrome. This included a scene in which the whole company appeared on the deck of a cruise ship in the Mediterranean on which whistles had just been blown to signal a life boat drill.

During one performance Jack had a spot of bother with the straps of his life jacket and couldn't move his arms. The 'Officer' in charge of the drill came to his aid but in his struggles to extricate the leading man only managed to get himself caught up in the life jacket as well. This reduced the whole cast, not to mention the audience, to fits of helpless laughter. Indeed, the 'life jacket tangle' was obviously such a popular addition to the show that it was kept in for the rest of the run – over three hundred performances.

It can't have lost any of its spontaneity because people who saw the show right up to the last night used to delight in saying that they'd been to see *Stand Up and Sing* the night that Jack Buchanan got into such a tangle with his life-jacket!

The year of 1925 brought an important milestone in Noël Coward's career with the revue *On With the Dance*, when he worked for the first time in collaboration with the celebrated London impresario, C.B. Cochran – 'Cocky' to his friends, and not infrequently cocky to his adversaries.

Between this highly successful show and the next he wrote for Cochran, Coward suffered the two severest maulings from public and press in his career, with the failure of both *Home Chat* and *Sirocco*. The morning after the vitriolic reception of *Sirocco*, Coward suggested to Cochran that it might be better if he didn't complete the revue, to spare Cochran the fateful road down which his career seemed to be heading.

But Cochran was shrewd. He knew Coward and he knew that what he next wrote would be guaranteed to win back his popularity and to restore him to the pinnacle of the London stage. He told him to press ahead with the revue, which came to be called *This Year of Grace* and was filled with delightful songs such as 'A Room With a View', 'Dance, Little Lady' and 'Lorelei'.

Unlike *On With the Dance*, in which Cochran insisted that Coward should work with other composers and writers, *This Year of Grace* was entirely his own work

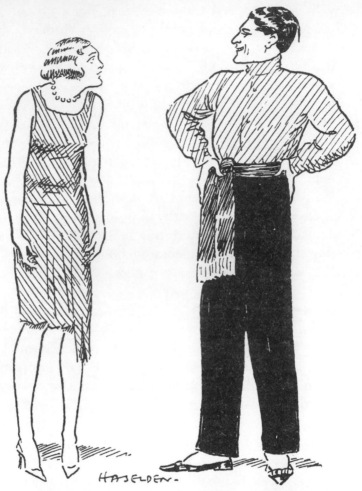

DRESSED TO KILL; OR, OMNIA VINCIT IVOR.

Lucy Griffin . . . . . Miss Frances Doble.
Sirio Marson . . . . . Mr. Ivor Novello.

from start to finish. With his tireless appetite for work, he threw himself into the book, the music and the lyrics – and then set about directing the show. There was scarcely an area of the production in which he didn't take a close personal interest.

There were no fewer than eight hundred dresses to be chosen for the revue and, in the middle of rehearsals, Coward found himself spending a whole day at the Apollo Theatre watching a parade of these pass across the stage. Even so, he knew exactly what he wanted and when he saw Maisie Gay dressed for one of her numbers in a black satin dress with a waistcoat, he found the effect not to his liking and asked for the costume to be changed.

The show opened in Manchester to enthusiastic delight. However, Cochran still wanted to make a few changes, among them a completely new comedy scene for Miss Gay. What's more, he wanted to advertise it for the Monday night performance and was asking Coward for it only three days in advance. Coward said that he was worn out, and drained of ideas, but Cochran just answered that he wanted something by the end of the weekend, and something good.

The following day Cochran got a call; Coward had an idea. On the next day, the Sunday, he was up in Manchester trying it out on stage with Cochran and Maisie Gay. By the Monday night it was in the show and was a howling success. The sketch was called 'Bus Rush' and involved Miss Gay in speaking just one word. After trying in vain to clamber on to a bus during the rush hour she finally gave in and shouted 'Taxi!'

Cochran hadn't achieved his own success without his own fine sense of the theatre In his case, he had a special way with the theatrical press. Before the opening of *This Year of Grace* he sent out a press notice of sorts, which read:

My revue, being by Noël Coward, will, I imagine, be

booed and if I accord the Press their usual invitation, they will doubtless tear the show to bits and deny any merit in book, lyric or music.

Cochran also knew a thing or two about London first night audiences and charged thirty shillings for a seat in the stalls, based on the reasoning that the show was really written for the more receptive and intelligent audiences that would start appearing after the third night. To a journalist who challenged him with this assumption about the lack of intelligence of his first night patrons, Cochran answered, 'What other explanation is there for their willingness to pay thirty shillings for a stall?'

'They think it worth the money to sit near the critics,' replied the journalist.

'Doesn't that prove what I said?' answered Cochran with a smile.

Whatever Cochran's opinion of theatrical critics, they were almost unanimous in their praise of *This Year of Grace*. In fact, the story circulated for some time that one well-known dramatic critic had been spotted leaving the London Pavilion in a shifty manner one Saturday afternoon. When asked what he was up to, he was forced to admit ashamedly that he had been to *buy* two tickets for Coward's show, 'one for myself and one for my wife'.

Of all the melodies in this new show 'A Room With a View' won immediate and lasting popularity, thanks to its charming performance by Sonnie Hale and Jessie Matthews – albeit one that resulted from a not inconsiderable struggle at times during rehearsals. Jessie Matthews suffered an acute anxiety to succeed which produced some curious over-elocution, particularly in the line 'High above the mountains and sea'.

From his seat in the stalls Coward stopped the song at this point and asked scathingly, 'How do you spell "mountain", Jessie?'

'M-o-u-n-t-a-i-n,' she answered.

'How do you pronounce it, dear?'

'"Mountain".'

'Then for God's sake *sing* "mountain" and not "mountayn",' he replied caustically.

This difficulty sorted out, the audience adored the song. The Prince of Wales was so taken with it that he asked for the tune to be played no fewer than nine times at a ball he attended in Egham in aid of the King Edward VII Hospital.

Jessie Matthews's nervousness extended to the opening night at the London Pavilion, where Coward was able to watch the opening scenes before his own curtain up an hour later in *The Second Man*, then running at the Playhouse. Coupled with the demands of the show, she had personal anxieties away from the stage and collectively this had her shaking in the wings as she waited for her first entrance. The cue came, and she was on stage starting to dance when she went into her first high kick and, to everyone's amazement, fell into a crumpled heap.

Up in his box with Cochran, Coward, head in hands, dared not look, convinced that Jessie Matthews had broken her ankle and was out of the show.

'She's all right,' Cochran assured him.

'Is she up?'

'She's up.'

'Is she dancing?'

'She's dancing,' Cochran told him. Coward nervously watched the show quickly pick itself up and romp towards the glorious triumph of 'A Room With a View' near the end of the first half.

Four years after *The Year of Grace* Noël Coward brought *Words and Music* to the stage, first to the Opera House in Manchester and subsequently to the Adelphi. Although this was not the box-office success that *This Year of Grace* had been, *Words and Music* was richly endowed with both and brought with it at least a couple of songs at the high-water mark of Noël Coward's compositions: 'Mad About the Boy' and 'Mad Dogs and Englishmen'.

One of the other numbers, 'Something to Do with Spring', attracted less favourable attention on the opening night with its line, 'I'd love to know what that stallion thinks, maybe it's something to do with Spring'. This was considered to be much too hot for public entertainment and had to be dropped after the first performance!

For over a dozen years Noël Coward turned his attention away from revue in London; 1939 saw *Set to Music*, but that was a Broadway show which included a number of pieces from earlier successes.

Then came the war, with different demands on his talents as both writer and performer. In the case of the latter he had to call on all his resources when playing to audiences very different to those who had cheerfully paid to see and hear him in peacetime.

Near the end of the war he found himself in one particularly tricky situation in Paris, where the US forces newspaper *Stars and Stripes* appeared with a scathing review of Coward's book *Middle East Diary*. In this he had made the unfavourable comment that at least one American hospital he had visited had been full of 'snivelling little boys from Brooklyn'.

'Kick this bum out of the country' ran the headline in *Stars and Stripes*, which was read by just about every US serviceman in Paris on the day that Coward was due to open in a cabaret there. To make matters worse, Maurice Chevalier, who was having trouble persuading the Allies that he wasn't really a collaborator, and Marlene Dietrich, whom most of the troops were convinced was a German spy, were topping the bill with him at the Marigny Theatre.

David Niven, who happened to be in Paris on leave, went backstage to see Coward before the show to warn him that the audience might be a trifle hostile and asked him how he was going to handle the situation.

'First I shall calm them, and then I shall sing them some of my very excellent songs,' answered Coward.

His friend wasn't convinced that this would ensure his safety and said he would be standing by the exit to whisk him away just in case the situation turned ugly.

From there he watched Coward walk on stage to absolute silence and then address the house, 'Ladies and gentlemen and all you dear, dear snivelling little boys from Brooklyn.' This caught the audience completely off guard and gave Coward the perfect breezy knock-out he needed to have them rolling in the aisles. Maurice Chevalier and Marlene Dietrich must have breathed a few sighs of relief as well.

The return of peace brought Coward back to the West End with a new revue, *Sigh No More*, in which Cyril Ritchard scored notable successes with songs like 'I Wonder What Happened to Him' and 'Nina'. The former was the subject of a minor row between Ritchard and Coward, with the singer taking exception to what he regarded as an improper reference:

Whatever became old Keeling?
I hear that he got back from France
And frightened three nuns in a train in Darjeeling
By stripping and waving his lance.

He wanted Coward to remove the three nuns. Coward asked why, to which Ritchard replied that he found the line about them offensive because he had a cousin who was a nun.

'All right, then,' said Coward. 'Make it four nuns.'

Cyril sang 'Nina' at the seventieth birthday show for Coward. I'd met him earlier at a charity do and we'd compared notes on the Master. In my nervous way I'd admitted that I was more than a little in awe of the great man. But it came as a surprise to hear a performer of the stature and presence of Cyril Ritchard also admit, 'Noël frightens me to death. He's terribly intimidating and very impatient with people and he can cut you like that.' This did little to bolster my confidence in Coward's company, but it was an interesting insight into the spell he cast even in the upper echelons of the profession.

Graham Payn, one of Coward's closest friends in the last thirty years of his life, was in the company singing 'Matelot' and 'Wait a Bit Joe', still full of the energy (and surprises) that he had displayed at his first audition for Coward thirteen years earlier in *Words and Music*. He had been a fourteen-year-old boy soprano at the time and, as his mother had shrewdly counselled, threw everything into his brief routine under the Master's scrutiny, as there weren't many openings in revue for boy sopranos pure and simple. So, to Coward's amazement, the young lad sang 'Nearer My God to Thee' while doing a tap dance! Mind you, he got the job and made the first acquaintance of a lifelong friend.

In *Sigh No More*, Graham Payn was asked by Coward after one performance to give a little more charm to one of his numbers. The following night he really went to town with it and had barely finished and reached the wings when the pass-door flew open and Coward burst through to tell him witheringly, 'I said a little more charm wouldn't hurt – I didn't ask you to be *Mary Rose* on skates!'

Coward found other enthusiastic members of the cast a little disconcerting too. At the first dress rehearsal the young actor cast as the fourth harlequin bounded on to the stage wearing tights for the first time and manifestly unaware of what should be worn under them. In a piercing whisper Coward said to the choreographer, Wendy Toye, 'For God's sake, go and tell that young man to take his Rockingham tea service out of his tights.'

The same problem had arisen in even more alarming proportions fourteen years earlier in Cochran's *1931 Revue*, to which Coward had contributed a number of items. Among these was a number entitled 'City', which the tenor Bernardi was cast to sing against a futuristic backcloth. To add to the air of fantasy the costume designer had decided to dress him as a harlequin and, like the young dancer in *Sigh No More*, he appeared at the dress rehearsal sporting a pair of tights – red ones.

After the rehearsal Cochran's assistant, Frank Collins, came on stage to give notes to the cast and told Bernardi, 'Mr Cochran is delighted with the way you are singing the number, but he does feel that unless you wear a jock strap the audience may not be able to pay full attention to the lyrics.'

'But Mr Collins,' replied Bernardi in his broad Lancastrian tones, 'I was wearing one. I've got it on now, packed with brown paper!'

'I see,' said Collins, lowering his gaze fractionally. 'I'll tell Mr Cochran, but he's really quite concerned. He may suggest an operation.'

The Master himself wasn't beyond minor misunderstandings in the excitement of a successful show. Ten years after *Sigh No More*, he accepted the highly lucrative and much needed offer of a cabaret season at the Desert Inn, Las Vegas. There he was told by a friend one night that David Rose, a composer he much admired, was going to be at a ringside table to watch the show. Coward was thrilled at the prospect of meeting the creator of 'Holiday for Strings'. After finishing his first show, he asked where Rose was sitting, went to the table and, with his hands over the man's eyes, hummed through the entire chorus of 'Holiday for Strings'.

This was a charming gesture and one that was greatly appreciated by the recipient, especially as he didn't happen to be David Rose. In his enthusiasm the Master had gone to the wrong table!

Perhaps it was in the variety offered by revue that he was able to give fullest expression to his modest claim to 'a talent to amuse'. In any event the ghost of André Charlot, who had so summarily dismissed the young Coward, must have been eating humble pie somewhere in the eternal wings.

Tonight at 8.30

Even for an artist of Noël Coward's aplomb and self-confidence, opening nights could be a wretched ordeal. As a very young playwright with a string of precociously successful productions under his belt, he was perfectly set up for the critics when misfortune came knocking. Then they were able to dismiss his popular work as flashes of fleeting brilliance, and join dissatisfied audiences in condemning the failures.

The first two of these, *Home Chat* and *Sirocco*, came in 1927, a time when Coward was starting to work in closer collaboration with C.B. Cochran. But then Cochran himself was no stranger to hostile first nights.

In 1920 he brought Laurette Taylor back to the London stage in a new play by her husband J. Hartley Manners, *One Night in Rome*. Her arrival was eagerly awaited following her triumph on both sides of the Atlantic in 1912 in *Peg o' My Heart*, again written by her husband, in which she captivated audiences with her performance as the wondrously arch but staunchly loyal Peg.

This new role, of an Italian clairvoyant and widow of a cruel nobleman who had very sensibly shot himself, cast her in a different mood; one not guaranteed to win over the post-war London audience. The play itself was in for a rough ride, too.

The first hint of trouble came as the curtain rose on the opening scene, or rather rose only a third of its usual height. Barely had a few words of dialogue been spoken when the first of many voices called from the gallery, 'Raise the curtain. We can't see anything!'

Those whose seats did allow them a clear view of the stage peered into a dimly lit room, hung with purple drapes and littered with the paraphernalia associated with the mystic arts. It was all rather unsettling. To make matters worse, as so often happens when catastrophe is lurking in the wings, the script gave rise to a succession of unfortunate lines.

'What a charming room!' exclaimed one of the characters on making his entrance.

'We can't see it; raise the curtain!' yelled the gallery.

A little while later came another delicious *faux pas*, 'She makes it difficult for anyone to see her,' which was greeted by howls of derision which rose to a crescendo when another character commented, 'What a horrible room'.

All the same, when the curtain came down to close the first act, there were enthusiastic calls for all the principals.

'I'm awfully sorry about this,' said Laurette Taylor to the house, pointing to the curtain. 'In the next act we'll have it higher. The scenery was made in America, where we do things so small. We didn't know we were coming into a theatre so high.'

This was only a short-term truce, however. As soon as the curtain had risen on Act II the turmoil resumed and continued unchecked for half an hour.

'Shut up and go back to America!' yelled one voice, rising above the general pandemonium.

When one of the cast started playing the violin he was greeted with cat-calls and a shower of pennies. The next things to be thrown were stink bombs! The cacophony of sneezing and coughing which followed their arrival made it impossible to continue the performance.

Laurette Taylor tried to pacify the gallery by offering seats in the orchestra stalls the following night. Cochran joined her on stage and, taking her by the hand, attempted to speak to the house. But his star cut him off, saying in a faltering voice, 'It isn't like England for you to do this.'

'I have brought Miss Taylor, this great artist, so beloved, three thousand miles to appear here tonight,' continued Cochran. 'I will not allow her to appear here amid this scene of disorder. I have decided, therefore, to ring the curtain down and to dismiss this audience tonight.'

Several minutes of further commotion followed this announcement, during which the curtain yo-yoed up and down and Cochran exchanged words with various sections of the house who tried to persuade him that it wasn't their fault and they wanted the show to go on. He was adamant he was not going to subject Laurette Taylor and the rest of the cast to further indignity, however, and *One Night in Rome* closed its turbulent first night in London.

Over the next seven years London audiences grew accustomed to enjoying witty, sophisticated and above all highly successful works by Noël Coward. After all, he'd given them *The Vortex*, *Fallen Angels*, *Hay Fever* and *On With the Dance*. The prospect of a new Coward play in the autumn of 1927 seemed full of promise, so the failure of *Home Chat* came as all the more of a disappointment.

Coward himself wasn't sure the piece was up to scratch, but Basil Dean seemed keen to produce it and

ROBBING PETER OF HIS CHARACTER TO PAY OUT PAUL.

Janet Ebony . . . . Miss Madge Titheradge.
Peter Chelsworth . . . . . Mr. Arthur Margetson.

Madge Titheradge, for whom he had written the lead, liked the play, so it went into rehearsal and opened at the Duke of York's Theatre on 25 October – the anniversary of the Charge of the Light Brigade, another celebrated failure!

General agreement was that the plot was weak – or at least the first night audience expected Coward to come up with something a little more inspiring than a young married woman being found in the same railway car as an attractive male friend at three in the morning. Then there was the performance itself, in which Basil Dean's carefully rehearsed pauses were agonizingly prolonged by one of the elderly actresses in the cast who kept forgetting her lines, thereby bringing the play to a complete standstill at regular intervals.

'We expected better,' yelled a dissatisfied patron to Coward at the final curtain.

'So did I,' he replied.

And that just about summed up *Home Chat*, which closed after thirty-eight performances. The *Daily Mirror*'s reviewer picked up the fact that Coward had written the piece in a week and wrote that he wished Coward had allowed himself a fortnight, 'for then we might have had two good laughs during the evening instead of only one.' However, *Home Chat* was merely a curtain raiser for the rumpus which was destined to follow with *Sirocco* a month later.

Coward had written the play in 1921 and Basil Dean had long wanted to stage it. So, after a considerable amount of rewriting, it went into rehearsal soon after *Home Chat* opened, with Ivor Novello and Frances Doble taking the leads.

The plot concerned a bored young English wife, left alone in Italy by her husband, who falls madly for a dashing Italian waiter, runs off with him for a week and then throws off both Romeo and husband to set out on an independent life of her own. It was a more serious theme than had occupied Coward of late and the audience on the opening night didn't warm to it. Neither were the leads strong enough to sustain the parts Coward had written for them.

Ivor Novello's appearance in blue-striped pyjamas brought sniggers from the house. When the lovers kissed in the first act they were greeted by a chorus of giggles and sucking noises from the gallery. By Act Two, when passions were reaching their height, the audience was laughing out loud. Neither did the cast

help themselves. Frances Doble answered a lone voice
that cried from the gods, 'Give the old cow a chance',
by saying, 'Thank you, sir. You are the only gentleman
here.'

By the time the curtain fell at the end the
auditorium was in a state of sustained civil war. Cries
of 'Rubbish! Rubbish!' rained down from the gallery, in
reply to which Miss Doble's fans set up chants of
'Bunny! Bunny!', her popular nickname.

Basil Dean, who never went to his first nights, had
recently arrived from dinner and was standing at the
prompt corner smiling cheerfully and ringing the
curtain up and down in complete misunderstanding of
the furore that was coming from out front. Coward
soon dispelled his pleasure. Striding on to the stage he
walked straight to the centre of the line of actors
nervously drawn up to take the curtain and, with his
back to the audience, shook hands with Ivor Novello
and kissed Frances Doble's hand. The audience
erupted into even more strenuous cries of disdain.

Coward stood facing the unbelievable din for seven
minutes before it subsided enough for calls for Miss
Doble to be heard. In her confusion, and to the
unrestrained glee of all, she came forward and
announced, 'Ladies and gentlemen, this is the happiest
night of my life.' Coward heard Ivor Novello giggle at
this and couldn't restrain himself from starting to
laugh too. Once again there were roars of vengeful
mirth from the audience. From then on the evening
descended into pandemonium. The company looked
stunned and dazed. Frances Doble appeared to be close
to fainting and had to be helped off stage. Coward was
railed and spat at as he left the theatre and the
orchestra made their own contribution to the chaos by

striking up with 'God Save the King'.

Raymond Massey, who was there for the opening, recalled seeing at least three separate fist fights in different parts of the house.

Smash hits weren't without their opening night hitches, too. *Cavalcade*, with all its full theatrical splendour, almost literally ground to a halt in the big scene in which a troopship set sail for the Boer War in South Africa. This was contrived mechanically by large platforms, one sliding under the other. With the excitement and nervousness of the first night, the crowd waiting to come on for the following scene mounted the second platform too early, causing the one with the troopship to stick fast.

Up in the Royal Box Coward was told that it might be fixed in a couple of minutes – or a couple of hours. He sat there impassively as the curtain stayed down, with a fixed smile glued to his face and tiny beads of perspiration dripping from his chin, until the curtain finally rose on the next scene after an agony of waiting in the house and feverish levering and straining backstage.

Having experienced anxious opening nights himself, Coward was obviously sensitive to the misgivings felt by friends awaiting curtain up on a new production. While Evelyn Laye was nervously making up for the first night of *Bitter Sweet* in New York, Coward knocked at her dressing-room door and came in with a small packet which he put on her dressing-table, asking her to unwrap it there and then. Inside, she found a delightful little silver box.

'Just press the button,' Coward told her, and when she did so a mechanical bird appeared, flapping its wings and singing.

'I wanted to be the first to give you the bird,' said Coward with a broad grin as he hurried away.

It was the sort of joke which could have backfired horribly, but coming from Coward it broke Evelyn Laye's tension perfectly.

He enjoyed giving first night presents. When *Private Lives* opened at the Phoenix Theatre on 24 September 1930 Coward gave a little silver book entitled *Private Lives* to several of his friends. On the cover was a specially written inscription; when this was touched, the book opened to reveal a cigarette lighter.

Once that first brilliant production and subsequent tour of *Private Lives* (including its Broadway run) had ended, Gertrude Lawrence, whose own performance had contributed immeasurably to the play's success, found herself in a play by Clemence Dane, along with three or four other actors of similar status and a producer worthy of such a cast. The management of the play was the responsibility of a twenty-three-year-old man, almost utterly unknown in the profession at the time but soon to establish himself in the forefront of London impresarios – Hugh 'Binkie' Beaumont.

The show opened in Bournemouth. The first night moved smoothly to its final curtain without obvious mishap and the principals were invited to supper with Mr Beaumont afterwards. There they tucked into delicious fare, drank champagne enthusiastically and looked ahead to a successful and enjoyable run.

With the coffee, however, came a mild astringent, so mild that with less sensitive players it might have passed unnoticed. In terms of great delicacy but shrewd and penetrating accuracy, Binkie Beaumont started to pull the performance apart. The production, he felt, was perhaps a little 'conventional', a polite euphemism for crushingly boring. He detected that Miss Lawrence had seemed just the slightest bit 'hesitant' at times, meaning that she had better sharpen up on her lines pronto. And so he continued, delivering telling yet gentle reprimands wherever they were needed and leaving his guests, all of whom were at least ten years his senior, in no doubt as to who was running the show and, more importantly, paying their wages.

Fourteen years later there was another opening surprise in store for Gertie Lawrence across the Atlantic in Boston. She was playing Eliza Doolittle to the Henry Higgins of Coward's old friend Raymond Massey, with whom he had first appeared in *The Second Man* in 1928. This production of *Pygmalion* later transferred to the Ethel Barrymore Theater in New York, where it broke the house records for non-musical productions with a total of 179 performances. However, the first out-of-town performance in Boston ended in shambles.

Until the closing minutes, possibly even the final minute, of the play everything had gone better than cast or director had dared hope. From rehearsals they knew they were on to a winning production and Gertrude Lawrence was already acclaimed as the best Eliza any in the cast had ever seen; in many respects the part suited her perfectly, as Coward would doubtless have readily agreed.

Then, just as Eliza was about to make her final tumultuous exit, the curtain was lowered three times – prematurely! The first time it very nearly came all the way down to the stage, before hurtling back into the flies. A few seconds later it reappeared halfway and then slipped slowly back above the stage, as if hoping to pass unnoticed. Its final appearance was like the dipping of an ensign.

Needless to say, the result was disastrous. Eliza's exit and the vital last lines with Higgins were lost in the curtain's yo-yoing and when the play ended Raymond Massey was then left alone on stage without the curtain coming in on its correct cue to end the play.

That opening night also witnessed Gertrude Lawrence showing unaccustomed restraint on stage at the moment when Shaw directs Eliza to throw Higgins's slippers at him. In spite of pleading from Raymond Massey that she should try to hit him, or come breathtakingly close, she persisted throughout rehearsals in throwing them wide of the mark. On the opening night there was a sigh of disappointment from the house when she again failed to make contact – not that this state of affairs was to last.

When the play had settled down in its Broadway run and Raymond Massey had ceased watching for the slipper and dodging, or pretending to dodge, out of its way, Miss Lawrence's tomboy instinct overcame her discretion and she sent the slipper flying one night with deadly accuracy right at Higgins's nose. A cheer went up from the auditorium, but the look of amazement on Raymond Massey's face made her drop the second slipper and cry in horror, 'Oh! I've hit you.' At this he burst out laughing, joining the audience in their delight. As he later observed, 'For a season afterwards I had to duck pinpoint pitching.'

Gladys Cooper was another of Coward's long-standing friends who could be guaranteed to add a certain excitement to an opening night – not always for the right reasons, as it turned out!

Although she and Coward had been friends for almost forty years they had never actually worked together until he enticed her back from America in 1951 to take the lead in *Relative Values*. For both of them, this was to be their first real success in the West End after a run of disappointments, but it was a success that was hard earned in rehearsal ... and later.

Come the opening in Newcastle, the cast were on tenterhooks waiting for the leading lady to miss one of the many lines that had somehow been eluding her throughout the whole rehearsal period. She never actually dried, but the gaps while she grasped for the next line played havoc with the careful symmetry of Coward's script.

Gladys Cooper herself gave every outward sign of perfect composure and sailed through that first night quite unaffected by the minor slips she continued to make. These lasted until perilously close to the first night in town at the Savoy Theatre. One night no fewer than twenty-eight mistakes by the leading lady were counted, including the delightful remark that instead of going into the 'study' she was off to the 'understudy'.

Like Edith Evans and many of Noël Coward's other friends and colleagues, Gladys Cooper refused to be word-perfect at the first run-through; Coward would reply that it wasn't the first run-through that he was worried about, it was the first night. In the case of *Relative Values* she had certainly given him good cause for anxiety.

Whatever the outcome of the London opening was to be, he had his moment of gentle amusement at her expense with the flowers he sent to her dressing-room. While they had been on the road a succession of terrible pictures of the leading lady had appeared in local papers up and down the country – all due to the dark make-up she had been wearing on stage, which did not photograph well. Inevitably one of these prompted an anonymous letter saying, 'You old hag, why don't you go back to America.'

On the night of the dress rehearsal she had sent away a photographer from one of the evening papers to avoid similarly unfortunate episodes in London, but Coward and Binkie Beaumont had been with her at the time and had been vastly amused when she explained what had happened. Consequently she opened the card with Coward's flowers the following evening and read his message of endearment, 'Why don't you go back to America, you old hag, and take my play with you!' In return for that she gave him a word-perfect perform-ance that won an enthusiastic ovation at the end.

Alas, the same wasn't true six years later when she opened at the Saville Theatre in the £30,000 extrava-ganza *The Crystal Heart*, which proved to be all too brittle. Among its many demands this show required its sixty-nine-year-old star to sing and dance, which she hadn't done a lot of since her days at the Gaiety half a century earlier. To compound her problems she had cracked a bone in her chest and went into the opening night on painkillers. It must have been almost a merciful release when it closed four performances later.

Just as Laurette Taylor had found with *One Night in Rome*, there were lines in *The Crystal Heart* that played right into the audience's hands. 'What a lovely afternoon,' remarked Dilys Laye at one point, no doubt dreading the inevitable rejoinder that came from somewhere in the house, 'Not a very lovely evening.'

GRANDPA'S SERMON—AN EYE-OPENER FOR BABY

Frank Gibbons . . . MR. NOEL COWARD

Very nearly thirty years earlier, Gladys Cooper had opened at the Playhouse alongside other Coward stalwarts such as Hermione Baddeley and Ernest Thesiger in a play called *Excelsior*, which was a kind of female version of *The Rake's Progress*. Also included in the cast was her sister Doris, cast as the maid.

Though she made no claims to stardom, Doris Cooper reckoned she was up to playing the maid and was understandably a little unnerved when she heard a definite hissing sound coming from the house as soon as she entered on the opening night. This was repeated in the next few performances and the point was reached when she had to ask a friend to sit in the audience and find out what the matter was and why she had turned everyone against her right from the start.

'It's all right,' her friend reported with relief after watching her scene and coming round immediately afterwards. 'They're not actually hissing you; it's just a lot of people whispering to each other, "That's Doris Cooper, Gladys Cooper's sister!"'

In 1960 Noël Coward's new play *Waiting in the Wings*, which tells the story of a group of elderly actresses living in a retirement home, got off to a rocky start for at least one of the cast, thus setting the seal on the rest of the production, which turned out to be accident prone. This was due in part to the advanced years of most of the cast, two of whom actually passed away during the London run and the tour that followed.

Accidents of a less permanent nature afflicted most of the others in one way or another and Marie Löhr became the first to suffer when she broke her arm on the opening night and had to go on in a sling to give a heroic performance. The accident had happened on her way to the theatre after she had popped into St Martin-in-the-Fields to offer up a prayer for the show's success. Perhaps the play's quotation from *Macbeth* persuaded the Good Lord to think otherwise. In any event she slipped on the wet steps as she was leaving.

'Couldn't she have chosen a church without any steps?' asked Coward, who later observed, 'No good turn goes unpunished.'

When it came to the opening night of *Sail Away* the following year, the company was to learn the awful wisdom that lies behind the theatrical caution about not acting with dogs. Midway through the first act Coward had written a tender scene, played on board ship by moonlight, in which Elaine Stritch, as the cruise hostess, was found exercising a dozen dogs. There Coward had her meeting a young playboy who had come in search of her, hoping for a few intimate words in private. It was an important scene, for on it hung the audience's appreciation of the love story that was to unfold as the play progressed. The young man's first line ran, 'We must be approaching land. There's a definite change in the air.' To which the cruise hostess replied, 'Soon you'll be able to see the lighthouse at Algeciras.'

Unfortunately it wasn't a lighthouse that was uppermost in her mind on the opening night. Just as the young man was about to enter one of the dogs was seized by a sudden attack of stage fright and relieved itself generously centre-stage. This brought predictable roars from the house, to which the playboy entered in some confusion. 'We must be approaching land. There's a definite change in the air,' he began, after the audience had settled. But this only brought another outburst of delighted laughter and accompanying applause. Distinctly unsettled by this, the actor had difficulty keeping a straight face. Elaine Stritch summed up the situation at once and, in an effort to bring the audience to heel and so let the scene develop as Coward intended, she tried ad-libbing until the hilarity subsided. 'I can't remember which one did that,' she commented, eyeing her pack. In hindsight, it wasn't perhaps the wisest line to choose. Once delivered, though, there was no turning back. To that first night audience the relationship between the cruise hostess and the young playboy was immediately established as being comic. Coward's carefully-structured romance and its closing scene of renunciation just before the end of the play were swept along in a tide of jocular good humour to the frustration of both cast and playwright, who knew even before the final curtain fell that the critics would be giving the play a hard time as a result.

Marti Stevens was another of Coward's American leading ladies to suffer an unscripted opening when she had a slight mishap in *High Spirits*, the musical version of *Blithe Spirit*, written by Hugh Martin and Timothy Gray, which had enjoyed a phenomenally successful run on Broadway for eight months before moving to London with a new cast. Marti Stevens had stepped in as Elvira at the last minute and learned the part in ten days before the out-of-town preview in Oxford. From there the show transferred to Manchester, where Coward caught up with it for the opening night.

Elvira's first entrance was made on a flying wire from a twelve-foot-high platform, following her first line, 'Good evening, Charles,' which was delivered through a microphone. In rehearsals and in the try-out this
had worked to perfection, but in Manchester the microphone had a short circuit.

'Good evening, Charles,' said Marti Stevens right on cue and, with a speed known only to electricity, a violent shock went straight down the steel attachment to the flying harness, down her neck and sent her sailing off the platform. After swinging backwards and forwards across the stage from side to side, she was dumped on her bottom in a crumpled heap and the scene slowly dragged itself back to life.

'I'm very proud of you,' said Coward, wagging his familiar admonitory finger, when he went back stage in the interval. 'You managed to play the first act of my little comedy tonight with all the lighthearted brilliance of Lady Macbeth.'

When it came to commenting on other people's work after first nights Coward was a past master of the telling quip. At the première of *The Lion in Winter* he soon tired of the long, slow tolling of bells with which the film opens.

'If it strikes twelve,' he whispered to his companion, 'I'll turn into a pumpkin.'

'If you do,' she answered, 'I'll ride home in you.'

The modern theatre seldom excited him. He went to David Storey's play about a rugby-league club, *The Changing Room*, and wasn't very taken with it. On the opening night the cast had been very alarmed when they heard the sound of guns being cocked all round the auditorium at one point in the play. On the succeeding nights there was the same frightening staccato of clicks at exactly the same moment, which had them well and truly rattled until someone spotted what was happening. At the time when the sound was heard they were taking off their shorts to wash after the match and the noise was being caused by people banging binoculars against their glasses as they strained for a closer view. Coward's only comment as he left the theatre was, 'I didn't pay three pounds fifty just to see half-a-dozen acorns and a chipolata.'

Then there was the time he went to see Arthur

Miller's autobiographical play *After the Fall* in New York. Claudette Colbert accompanied Coward to the opening night and sensed as they left that the Master might make his feelings only too clearly known. She tried steering him away from Miller, but this only resulted in his shouting across the heads of the crowd, 'I preferred *This Is Your Life* when it was a television programme.'

As one who had been on the receiving end of more than enough first night flak the opportunity to speak his mind must have been irresistible.

To close on a personal note, he came to visit me at the Prince of Wales Theatre, not on a first night as it happened, but during the run of the Feydeau farce which Binkie Beaumont had staged as *Cat Among the Pigeons*. I had received a collection of wonderful notices from the press which quite convinced me that I was the best farceur in England since Ralph Lynn!

Noël came round about a fortnight into the run, sat in my dressing-room and talked of the difficulties faced by English actors in playing French farce. I waited fairly confidently for unstinting praise for my great performance and at last he said, 'You know, you really are one of our greatest farceurs, because,' and he paused, while I thought, 'Here it comes, this is one for the autobiography.' ' ... Because,' continued Coward, 'you never ever hang about.' And that was all he said.

Bad times are just around the corner

WHILE OPENING NIGHTS offer excitements all of their own (and not always of the most welcome kind, as we've seen), one of the thrills of live theatre is the constant presence of the unexpected. Each performance is unique – which, in some cases, is just as well. Noël Coward was better equipped than many actors to deal with unforeseen eventualities, though there were times when even he was nonplussed.

After the successful run of *The Vortex* in London in 1924 the show was taken to America, where it opened in Washington DC. One evening, at a moment of great drama in the last act, Lilian Braithwaite as Coward's mother picked up a box of drugs and hurled them, as she did every night, out of the window. Unfortunately the technical crew in Washington hadn't been primed for this and one of them who happened to be passing the window as the box came sailing through caught it and chucked it back – straight into Lilian Braithwaite's hands!

She gave it one look and threw it off again with such force that accuracy was sacrificed to momentum and the box caught the edge of the window, breaking it clean off. This had the audience in fits of laughter and the stage manager had no option but to lower the curtain to start the act again.

The following year Coward took the part of Lewis

SANGER'S QUICK SUPPER-BAR.

Dodd in *The Constant Nymph*, playing opposite Edna Best as Tessa. At the close of the play she has a heart attack and Coward used to pick Miss Best up in his arms and carry her to her bed to die. Then he would throw open the window and utter the final and deeply moving line of the play, 'Tessa's got away. She's safe. She's dead.'

One night the play moved towards its heartbreaking conclusion, Coward lifted Edna Best on to her bed, threw open the window and lamented, 'Tessa's got away. She's safe. She's OW!' as the sash cord broke and the window came smashing down across the back of his hands. Tessa, only recently expired, sat bolt upright and the curtain fell to roars of laughter.

Sometimes the unexpected comes by courtesy of other members of the cast. Coward must have had no

THE TWO DISGRACES.

Paulina Sanger . . . . MISS HELEN SPENCER.
Teresa Sanger . . . . MISS EDNA BEST.

end of fun trying to corpse Laurence Olivier in *Private Lives* and Gladys Cooper shared his sense of humour on stage. The night of 1 April 1925 saw her in full impish flight. At the time she was playing the title role in *The Last of Mrs Cheyney* and, aided and abetted by the stage manager, Herbert Chown, she brought chaos to the performance that night.

Having supplied themselves with a variety of alternative props they proceeded to slip these surreptiously to the other totally unsuspecting members of the cast. Ronald Squire went to light his usual cigar and found it gave off little bangs as soon as the match touched the end. Violet Campbell took a hearty bite at her apple and ended up with a mouthful of soap. Other ladies in the cast bit into the nice sweet wafers they nibbled on stage only to find them filled with flannel, and anyone who tried to stir their cup with a spoon that night found it crumpled up in their fingers.

It wasn't long before the whole cast was in a terrible dither wondering which object would be the next to catch them out. Gerald du Maurier was the only one to have escaped unscathed but, guessing that he would be the victim sooner or later, he did his best to avoid opening a parcel that he felt sure must have been booby-trapped. In the end he couldn't delay it any longer and gingerly unwrapped the paper only to find the parcel completely harmless. With great relief he sat down in a chair right on to a cushion that gave out terrible squeaks.

At a later date the joke was on Gladys Cooper herself, even if unintentionally on this occasion. She was appearing in *The Letter*, during which there is flashback to a previous scene to show 'what really took place in the bungalow when the murder was committed'.

This is a very difficult effect to achieve on stage with an entire scene having to be changed back to an earlier one in every detail, and all in the space of a few seconds. While the props and furniture were being reset, Gladys Cooper was struggling back into the frock she'd been wearing in the previous scene, so that when the lights went up she'd be found seated in a chair near a table in a perfect recreation of what the audience had already seen.

One night she groped her way towards the table in the black-out but couldn't find the chair and sat down on the stage in pitch darkness to a very loud and uncomfortable bump. She didn't forget that and the stage crew never forgot the chair again!

It wasn't very often that Coward himself was responsible for unscripted debacles of this sort, though when he was they could be spectacular. In April 1930, while holidaying in Singapore, he treated an audience to one of these, when his phenomenal memory and total absorption in his work came to the aid of a touring company due to stage R.C. Sherriff's First World War classic *Journey's End*.

The actor cast as Stanhope, the lead, fell ill and to the astonished delight of the company Coward stepped willingly into the breach and was word perfect within three days. Rehearsals were restricted to one run-through on the afternoon of the first performance – in the best traditions of rep they were doing a different show each night. Even so, Coward managed to find time to contrive some business all of his own. Following the dress rehearsal he suggested to John Mills, playing Raleigh, the young officer who dies in the last scene, that they might essay a fresh move to heighten the poignancy of the final moments. Would he like to try it, Coward wondered?

Flattered and thrilled at even being invited to express an opinion, the young actor said he would. Coward's suggestion was that instead of exiting immediately from the dug-out to face the machine-gun fire, the barrage and the star-shells, he would pause at the foot of the steps, put on his tin helmet, and then walk downstage once more to take a final look at Raleigh's body before walking slowly back to the steps and continuing up them to his destiny. John Mills thought this a marvellous idea which would certainly add a special ingredient to the final curtain.

The last scene came. John Mills 'died' in Coward's arms. Then he heard Coward walk slowly upstage to the steps; heard him pause; heard him walk back. Holding his breath and knowing that every eye was on

Captain Stanhope, now bending over him, the last thing John Mills expected was a resurrection, but a sudden agonizing blow sent him sitting bolt upright with a loud scream. Staring down at him was Coward – bare-headed, his tin hat having fallen with some momentum directly on to the late lieutenant's unprotected privates.

Summoning up a second, albeit rather strangulated, death rattle, he fell back on the bed, waiting for the inevitable laughter from the house. There wasn't a murmur. The magic of the play had cast its spell and was soon repaid with long and enthusiastic applause. Only the critic from the *Straits Times* dared to share Coward's privately held opinion that he wasn't ideally suited to play the battle-hardened Stanhope.

In the months before the outbreak of the Second World War Rex Harrison was cast to play Leo in the first London production of *Design for Living*, the part that Coward himself had taken when the play had been first staged in America with the Lunts six years earlier. This production opened in Brighton and a week later came into town to the Haymarket Theatre, where it ran for six months before moving to the Savoy.

There is one point in the play where Leo has to change from tails to pyjamas and during one matinée Rex was in the middle of this when he had to answer an urgent call of nature and only reached the wings just in time for his cue. He went on as coolly as usual until he realized that everyone was staring at him in astonishment. Glancing down, he saw that he had put on the pyjama trousers back to front; the seat was hanging baggily at the front and what was at the rear left little to the imagination. The rest of the cast were convinced he had done it on purpose and were splitting their sides. He hadn't, of course, and wasn't very amused.

Alan Webb, who played Ernest Friedman in the same production, was once in a play when a fireplace on stage fell down and knocked him on to his face, leaving behind a perfectly blank wall which showed that there could obviously never have been a fireplace there at all. Later in Rex's career falling scenery very nearly put paid to him.

Interestingly it had been Noël Coward who had suggested Rex as a possible Professor Higgins when he himself had turned down the role in *My Fair Lady*. Although he never exhibited any outward disappointment, there must have been times when the financial rewards of that show must have seemed very desirable.

Rex got the part of course, and in the fullness of time was playing Higgins on Broadway, where one night two years into the run he was halfway through his song 'Accustomed to Her Face' when there was a thunderous crash right behind the frontcloth where he was performing. The force of this almost blew him into the footlights and a shower of splinters and large pieces of wood flew under the billowing cloth, littering the stage. Then there was complete silence.

The orchestra sat stunned in their seats. The conductor's arms were frozen and Rex had to call for a note to try and finish the song, which he did to rousing applause from the audience.

When he came off he found the back of the stage looking as if a bomb had hit it. In fact, one of the very heavy sets flown in earlier in the show had frayed a rope after two years of being hoisted up and down and had dashed itself to smithereens on the boards below. If it had fallen only a few minutes later it would have landed on the entire company drawn up for the curtain call.

Laurence Olivier suffered a similar nightmare up in the flies during the run of *The Critic* in 1945, which formed half of a memorable double-bill with *Oedipus Rex*. Olivier was playing Mr Puff and, as an eye-catching finish for the part, he'd devised an elaborate routine that had him whizzing up and down like a yo-yo. This began as Mr Puff was trying to sort out something in the flies. With his eyes fixed far above the stage, he inadvertently stepped across a scenery bar lying on the stage-floor, which a moment later was hoisted upwards, carrying Mr Puff astride it. Up in the flies Olivier changed horses, so to speak, and clambered into a swing-seat bearing a cut-out cloud. In this he was gently lowered towards the stage, only to be blown back up again by a violent explosion when he was a matter of feet from the boards. While the rest of the company scanned the flies to see what had happened to Mr Puff, the cloud swing-seat was pulled to one side of the stage, where Olivier scrambled out of it, grabbed hold of a rope and shinned down this to the stage-floor. In the meantime the cloud appeared before the audience – empty. This was followed by the closing of the curtains and as they came together Mr Puff was to be seen clinging to the right-hand one, whence he fell in a somersault towards the footlights (Olivier having climbed up the curtain by means of a rope-ladder).

As a routine it was a marvellous finale – until the night when disaster struck and Olivier grabbed the rope down which he was to shin from his swing-seat and found that it came away as he pulled on it. The rope hadn't been fastened up above! With only the thin wire supporting the swing-seat to cling onto, he had to hang precariously thirty feet above the stage while the fly-men fumbled with their maze of ropes to see which would lower him securely to the stage. Down he came eventually in full view of the audience, who at best must have thought it was only a rather weak bit of business.

On a lighter note, there's the account of the havoc a recalcitrant piece of scenery brought to a matinée performance Gertrude Lawrence was giving once at the Aldwych in Daphne du Maurier's 1949 play *September Tide*. She was on stage playing an important scene with Michael Gough, the actor taking the part of her son-in-law, who was about to dive from the balcony of their house into the harbour to retrieve a drifting boat. In his absence, the plot directed that Miss Lawrence should fetch some towels from a cupboard ready for his return, by then suitably saturated after immersing himself in a bath of warm water provided in the wings by Herbert, his dresser.

Unbeknownst to the two of them, on this particular afternoon one of the cleats securing the flats of the heavy set gave way. Grabbing Herbert, who was on station with his bath of water, the stage manager told him to hang on to the flat while he went to fetch the stage crew to make good the damage before the whole set collapsed. Herbert was a dresser of the old school and willingly lent a hand to save the show.

Meanwhile, back on stage, Michael Gough dived from the balcony on to a pile of mattresses and made his way to the bath of water. Gertrude Lawrence crossed to the cupboard, opened it as she had done on every one of the other two hundred or so perform-ances and looked inside for the towels. On this afternoon, however, she was in for a shock. In place of the towels she found Herbert!

As bad luck would have it he was clinging to the set immediately behind the door. The situation wasn't helped by the fact that he cut a rather eccentric figure that hot afternoon, dressed in pin-stripe trousers, collarless shirt and white tennis shoes. Combined with the small Hitler moustache which he sported the whole effect was quite startling. Nevertheless, the audience might have accepted it as a curious twist in the plot for the central character to find the Führer inside a cupboard in tennis shoes – as long as Gertie Lawrence didn't laugh. Unfortunately there was little hope of this.

Not only was she dumbfounded by seeing Herbert but, ever the gentleman, he gave a little bow and said, 'Good afternoon, Miss Lawrence' – and that would have been too much for any actress. It certainly finished Gertrude Lawrence, who just managed to close the door before starting to giggle uncontrollably.

In the interim Michael Gough had clambered out of the bath and climbed back over the balcony dripping wet. There he was met with the sight of Gertrude Lawrence lurching about the stage as she struggled to regain control of herself and a gale of laughter from the audience. His spontaneous reaction was to check his flies.

Finding that they were in order he started delivering his lines but, receiving no response from Gertie who had collapsed to the floor by this time, spoke her lines too in a desperate effort to keep the plot moving. He also needed a towel and made for the cupboard, which brought further hoots of delighted glee from the audience, hoping to renew their brief acquaintance with Herbert. When he opened the door the cupboard was empty, which as far as he knew it was at every performance, so it wasn't until the act had struggled to its conclusion and they were off stage that he was able to find out just what had been going on while he had been in the bath.

Maurice Denham went through similar torment in the 1949 production of Coward's play *Fallen Angels* at the Ambassadors Theatre. As Willy Banbury, he had to play an angry scene in the second act with Hermione Baddeley, who had been cast as Julia Sterroll. At one point he had to storm to the door and shout, 'Have you seen this man since we were married?' However, on the night in question the drama of the scene rather got the better of his concentration and he turned on Miss Baddeley and furiously demanded 'Have you married this man since we were seen?' Audience and leading lady started giggling.

'Has this man seen we were married?' Denham tried again, hazarding a second attempt. 'Oh dear, no!' he then blurted out, by now irretrievably lost.

The audience were laughing out loud and Hermione Baddeley was so far beyond control herself that she left the stage to regain her composure and allow Maurice Denham to do likewise. In this they were impressively successful.

After taking a deep breath, Denham turned to the now mournfully serious leading lady as she re-entered and delivered his next line flawlessly, 'I'm terribly sorry for what I said just now.' At that they gave up any pretence; cast and audience roared in hilarious unison.

Two years earlier Kenneth More had had a more intimate experience of getting his lines crossed with the Master.

Like many young actors, he was greatly in awe of

meeting the Master for the first time and when the opportunity arose he was appearing at the Fortune Theatre in a highly acclaimed but poorly attended production of a play by Michael Clayton Hutton, *Power Without Glory*. This coincided with an unseasonably warm spell of spring weather and the Fortune wasn't exactly living up to its name when it came to enticing audiences inside its doors.

The call boy brought him the message that 'Mr Coward' wanted him on the telephone. 'Mr Coward ... you don't mean *Noël* Coward?' he asked. When the boy confirmed this, Kenneth trooped nervously after him to the stage door phone, down which he heard the inimitable voice inviting him to call round after the show. Coward was appearing as Garry Essendine in *Present Laughter* at the Haymarket and told Kenneth, 'I think I've got something that will interest you.'

Later that evening, his make-up hastily cleaned from his face after a performance from which by his own admission his mind had been more than a little absent, the young actor knocked nervously at the door of the star's dressing-room. It opened and Coward greeted him wearing a blue and white polka dot silk dressing gown.

Inside, they shared a plate of smoked salmon sandwiches and a thermos of tea while Coward outlined the plot of his new play, *Peace In Our Time*, which dealt with Britain after a German victory and occupation. To Kenneth's intense pleasure, Coward had been one of the few who had ventured inside the Fortune to see *Power Without Glory* and, liking what he had seen, was offering him the part of George Bourne, leader of the British resistance in his new play. Kenneth left with a copy of the script and an invitation to Coward's flat in a few days' time after he had had time to read through the play.

At this second meeting the atmosphere was more intimate. His host had donned the silk dressing gown, the lights were low, the fire glowed and Coward sat at the piano after dinner playing a selection of his own music. His guest took a seat by the fire, worried how the evening might end.

When Coward finished playing, he stood up and started walking slowly towards Kenneth, which quite unnerved the young actor. Jumping to his feet, he stammered, 'Oh, Mr Coward . . . I could never have an affair with you, because . . . because . . . you remind me of my father!'

Coward paused, his face perfectly inscrutable. Then he broke into a broad smile, said, 'Hallo, son,' and roared with laughter.

After that, they remained the best of friends!

Peace In Our Time also introduced Kenneth More to another friend, Elspeth March, who appeared in Coward's play as the novelist Janet Braid and won special mention from the *Daily Telegraph*'s reviewer for the two magnificent tirades she delivered in the play. Four years later she appeared as the nurse Fateesha in the production of Shaw's *Caesar and Cleopatra* which Laurence Olivier and Vivien Leigh staged, along with Shakespeare's *Antony and Cleopatra*, as their contribution to the Festival of Britain.

In the play Elspeth March wore a false nose and in one unhappy performance this was sent flying when Vivien Leigh went to slap her nurse's cheek but caught her on the nose by mistake. All was not lost. With remarkable agility, Vivien Leigh fielded it deftly with her other hand and was able to give it back to Elspeth

March, who exited holding her hand to her face
without the audience ever realizing that anything had
gone awry.

Unfortunately Vivien Leigh was less lucky during a
performance of *Titus Andronicus* when Noël Coward was
in the audience. She was playing the part of Titus's
daughter Lavinia who, after being ravished by the
lecherous sons of Tamora, has her tongue cut out and
her hands cut off to prevent her revealing the identity
of her attackers. However, she does manage to identify
them by clasping a staff in her forearms and scratching
the names of Demetrius and Chiron in the dust. The
trouble was that the night Coward went to see the
play, Vivien Leigh dropped the staff.

'Butterstumps!' he chided, wagging his finger in her
dressing-room after the show.

Brief Encounter, December 1945

[*Brief Encounter*

RESPECTABILITY'S LAPSE

Laura . . . . CELIA JOHNSON

She didn't fare much better one evening before the war in a production of *A Midsummer Night's Dream* in Regent's Park, in which she starred with Robert Helpmann. That night several members of the Royal Family came to see the show and at the end of the performance the two principals gave a special bow to the royal party. As they paid their respects, however, their elaborate head pieces became locked together and refused to budge. Stuck in this position like a pair of stags, they didn't have any option but to nestle close together and back off stage grinning foolishly at their royal patrons as they left.

Another of Coward's favourite leading ladies, Lynn Fontanne, had a spot of costume bother in the 1952 production of Coward's romantic comedy *Quadrille* at the Phoenix Theatre in London. She was playing a scene with Joyce Carey during one performance when, rising from a chair, she brought a small cushion with her, caught up on her bustle. This proceeded to bob up and down as she moved and in spite of Miss Carey's frantic efforts to remove it, Miss Fontanne, who didn't like being touched, managed to elude her. Joyce Carey had to leave the stage before she could get to the offending cushion and Lynn Fontanne remained alone to do a little dance, while the cushion bounced up and down in cheerful unison. The audience were delighted and when she came off stage she commented, 'You know, that scene's never got so many laughs.'

In the following year, Coward celebrated the Coronation in 1953 by playing King Magnus in Shaw's play *The Apple Cart*. George Rose was in the cast too and one night suffered the awful embarrassment of halitosis, to Coward's unbridled delight. Before the show George had cheerfully indulged in *moules marinières* but had no idea that the garlic lingered so long or so powerfully on his breath until he started playing his scene with Coward. The Master caught the first powerful whiff, backed away in horror and muttered, 'Don't breathe out, you'll scorch the furniture polish.' This was spoken as an aside, but was clearly audible. It threw George considerably and, just as he was recovering his composure, Coward added, 'We only need a little bread, and then we could all have a meal.' That finished George off completely.

This was also the year in which Coward wrote *After the Ball*, which was first produced by Robert Helpmann in 1956. The two of them teamed up later to play Sebastien in *Nude with Violin*, Coward taking the part in America and Helpmann stepping in to succeed Michael Wilding in London.

Coward had written Sebastien for himself but later adapted the part to suit John Gielgud, who opened in the role and played it for seven months until he had to leave for an engagement at Stratford, at which point Michael Wilding succeeded him. Gielgud also directed the production and came down from Stratford for a week to rehearse with Robert Helpmann before he opened, setting the scene for a classic Gielgud brick. Throughout that week of rehearsals he gave notes to all the rest of the cast, who had been playing their parts for ages, but never said a word to the new Sebastien. Only at the final rehearsal before his opening did Gielgud pass any comment. 'I think you're absolutely marvellous, Bobby, the way you've done it in the time. It's absolutely extraordinary. Of course I could never have played it like that. You see, I'm a straight actor.'

'I've been waiting for that one the whole week,' replied Helpmann.

In 1956, Noël Coward became a tax exile for a time leading to the publication of this Ronald Searle cartoon and the accompanying verse in *Punch* magazine:

I'll Never See You Again

*W*HERE the remote Bermudas ride,
    He who once sang of "London
    Pride"
Descended from a westbound 'plane
And rais'd a breathless, cultured strain:
"What should I do but sing the praise
Of this entirely splendid place
Where my design for living's free
Of all responsibility?
For see how present laughter thrives
In our expatriated lives:

Here, wafted in on every breeze,
Come cavalcades of royalties,
Which gather in my bank in stacks
Unravag'd by the income tax!
So by this venture I am freed
From thraldom to that happy breed
Who in the island of their birth
Still work, and pay, for all they're
    worth.
Now a new loyalty I'll own
In which we serve ourselves alone."

                            B. A. Y.

'Oh my God,' said Gielgud, 'I didn't mean that . . .'

Sir John had also starred in and directed the original production of Christopher Fry's *The Lady's Not For Burning* and much of the success of that famous original production was due to his vigilant attention to detail, which kept everyone in the company on their toes right through the long run. Occasionally his ideas allowed him to become a little carried away, sometimes with unexpected consequences.

There was one evening when he decided that everyone hidden behind the door in the second act should burst out with considerably more dash and flair, making up spontaneous exclamations as they rushed on. The rest of the cast weren't as convinced as Sir John that this was a good idea and suggested a rehearsal. He dismissed that idea; it would spoil the excitement.

As it turned out there was no shortage of that. The mass entrance was catastrophic. Harcourt Williams and Eliot Makeham quite independently came out with the same boisterous remark, which had the two of them in hysterics. In his enthusiasm Peter Bull bumped into Richard Leech, who collided heavily with Pamela Brown and sent her sprawling to the floor, only a minute or two before the script directed her to collapse in a dead faint. Meanwhile Richard Burton had stopped scrubbing the floor and was staring in horror at his fellow players as if they had just had a collective brainstorm.

'Sorry, chaps, entirely my fault,' admitted Sir John as the curtain fell and they all collapsed in helpless laughter.

There were a lot of unscripted laughs in the course of that production, as it happened. There was the night when Esmé Percy lost his glass eye on stage in his big scene and let out the distraught whisper, 'Do be careful, don't tread on it, they cost eight pounds each.' Richard Leech, a doctor as well as an actor, eventually retrieved it for him, but the episode sewed an idea in his mind and that of Richard Burton.

A collection of glass eyes was purchased and together they hid these liberally all over the set and inside props. At the next performance, the cast were greeted by the unsettling gaze of dozens of glass eyes that met them at every turn. There were glass eyes in the bottom of goblets, inside purses and rolling around the stage like marbles. The lady may not have been for burning, but Richard Burton was in for a bit of a grilling after that.

So, too, was Marcia Warren, one of the most recent of Coward's Madame Arcatis, after a perfectly inno-cent but no less calamitous episode during her days as a stage manager in rep. One night she took up the curtain prematurely in an interval of an Agatha Christie thriller to reveal to an aghast audience the whole cast on stage, including several corpses, enjoying a refreshing cup of tea!

Noël Coward made his final stage appearance in his trilogy *Suite in Three Keys* at the Queen's Theatre in 1966. He had been ill for some time and, as a result of the drugs he was taking, for once in his career dried from time to time. It might have been a sad coda to a long and dazzling career, but Coward carried off any small shortcomings with his characteristic fortitude.

He played a dinner party scene with Lilli Palmer right down on the apron of the stage and used to whisper to her behind the salad in moments of forgetfulness, 'What's my line?' and she would whisper it back. After a while he grew bolder and would ask 'What?', making her repeat it and enjoying the delicious fun of knowing that the audience never noticed and were still eagerly flocking to see him as they had done for half a century.

Hands across the sea

IT WAS THE admiration of success that Noël Coward instinctively recognized in America and the Americans he had met in London that first persuaded him to set sail for the New World in the spring of 1921, with a one-way ticket on the *Aquitania*, less than £20 in his pocket and a brain boiling over with ideas.

That first visit couldn't in all honesty be counted a commercial triumph, beyond the fact that he did manage to eke out an existence by selling a few articles to *Vanity Fair* and some short stories to *Metropolitan*. What it did achieve was far and away of greater significance; in New York Coward met similarly minded members of the American theatre with whom he was to form life-long friendships as they rose together to international fame.

Among the first of these new acquaintances was a golden-haired fire-cracker of an actress from Alabama, the daughter of a Congressman and grand-daughter of a Senator – Tallulah Bankhead. She was witty, vivacious and relished the daring and outrageous – characteristics that were hallmarks of her career. She also had a wonderfully cavalier attitude towards her chosen profession.

About a year before she met Coward, she opened in *Footloose* in the Greenwich Village Theatre in New York and one day walked in to see her friend Ann Andrews, who was appearing in *The Hottentot* at the George M. Cohan Theatre. Miss Andrews was pleased to see her, though a little surprised at the visit on a Wednesday afternoon. 'What's happened?' she asked. 'It's only three thirty! Why aren't you at your play?'

Tallulah Bankhead felt a certain weakness in her knees as she realized that she had walked off the stage at the end of the first act, quite convinced that the play had just finished!

Minor details like this aside, she soon established herself as a promising actress on the American stage and crossed the Atlantic three years later to appear with Gerald du Maurier in *The Dancers*, in which she scored a sensational triumph.

In 1925 Basil Dean promised her the part of Sadie Thompson in Somerset Maugham's play *Rain* when it opened in London, subject to the author's agreement. Unfortunately the author didn't agree and, having learned the lines, Tallulah Bankhead found herself sacked at the second rehearsal. To add to her misery and fury, she heard rumours that Olga Lindo had been given the part instead before Basil Dean was able to break the news to her in person. The weather added its own ironic commentary by summoning up a deluge and the spurned actress took a handful of aspirins and waited for the end.

She was woken the next morning by an anxious Noël Coward on the telephone asking if she could learn the part of Julia Sterroll in his new play *Fallen Angels* in four days? Margaret Bannerman, who had been cast to play opposite Edna Best, had pulled out and Coward was in a jam.

'Learn it in four days?' exclaimed Tallulah. 'I'll do it in four hours!'

'What's your salary?' enquired Coward, getting down to business.

'One hundred pounds a week.'

'But you were only getting forty pounds in *Rain*.'

'That's true, but I wanted to play Sadie Thompson. I don't give a goddam if I play this or not.'

'Agreed, if you can open on Tuesday.'

'I'll open it on Tuesday, or I'll fix it so no one else will ever be able to open in it.'

The next day she received a chit from Somerset Maugham and one hundred pounds. It took her four days to compose the reply that she sent back with the money.

In the meantime she fulfilled her promise and was word-perfect come the opening night, although she did allow herself one small deviation from Coward's script. In place of his line, 'Oh dear, rain' she couldn't resist substituting, 'My God, rain!' and the audience roared their approval. They were pretty enthusiastic about *Fallen Angels*, too. The same could not be said of Somerset Maugham's play. When it opened both *Rain* and Olga Lindo died the death. In the case of any actress other than Tallulah Bankhead it might have been reasonable to say that virtue had had its own reward!

Fallen Angels established her as a popular if unconventional star of the West End stage and, together with other members of the bright theatrical set that seemed to embody the Roaring Twenties, she was soon making her presence felt all over London.

One night she hauled Beatrice Lillie out of her hotel bed at one in the morning to attend a party she was giving. Bea went over by taxi, still wearing her nightgown, and was soon fast asleep once again on

"I WISH HE WOULDN'T CALL US 'FALLEN'; IT'S SO DÉMODÉ!"

"YES; AND 'ANGELS' TOO—SO VICTORIAN!"

Jane Banbury	MISS EDNA BEST.
Julia Sterroll	MISS TALLULAH BANKHEAD.

Tallulah's bed, where she stayed until six. Tallulah took her friend back to the Savoy once the revels had ended and, realizing that the hall porter might think it a little odd to be admitting two ladies at that time in the morning, one of them in her night attire, Miss Bankhead decided to pull rank. Attempting to use her friend's title, she demanded, 'Give me Lady Keel's pee.'

The man appeared not to have heard, so she repeated, 'Lady Keel's pee, please,' and Miss Lillie chimed in with, 'My pee, my good man, my pee!'

In the autumn of 1928 the two of them were invited by C. B. Cochran to attend one of the afternoon revivalist meetings that were being held in the Albert Hall by the American spiritualist and preacher Aimée Semple McPherson. This redoubtable lady had come to these shores with a mission to redeem the British, and under the auspices of the Four Square Gospel Churches of the British Isles was packing them in afternoon after afternoon. The two actresses were fascinated by her piety and were determined to test whether it was genuine or part of a convincing performance. They invited Miss McPherson for a drink, which she parried by asking them to visit her the next day at her hotel.

They took Leslie Howard along with them, but no drinks were served that afternoon: Miss McPherson entertained them with slides of her temple.

All the same, she was fascinated by Beatrice Lillie's wit and went that night to watch her and Noël Coward in their final rehearsal of *This Year of Grace* before the production set sail for America.

She was with Tallulah Bankhead the following night at an impromptu party the actress had thrown for theatrical friends, all of whom had been primed to confess to trespasses and peccadillos in the hope that Miss McPherson might come clean about a few skeletons in her own cupboard.

What was preying most on her mind, however, was the thought that she hadn't said goodbye properly to Beatrice Lillie before she left for Southampton to board the *Leviathan* for the voyage to New York. She wanted to give Bea an autographed Bible and when Tallulah rather flippantly suggested driving down to catch the ship, Aimée Semple McPherson jumped at the idea.

Thick fog delayed them on the road, though it also prevented the *Leviathan* from sailing, so Miss Lillie got her Bible. However, it also resulted in their returning to London at two in the afternoon, hours after Miss McPherson should have been at a meeting with her sponsors.

In the car on the way back to London it had been agreed that no one would tell where they had been or what they'd been up to. This was fine in theory, but the press were given several differing accounts of what had gone on which resulted in a page one headline in the *Daily Express,*

Miss McPherson's all night Motor Journey.
Actress friends of the Evangelist.
Reticence of her companions.

At the first whiff of scandal the 'evangelist' fled north to Glasgow, leaving the mystified Secretary of the Four Square Gospel Churches trying to explain to reporters that Miss McPherson had presumably regarded the actresses as a couple of good catches.

There were others who thought the whole thing was a put-up job by C. B. Cochran to grab a little free publicity for *This Year of Grace* prior to its American opening!

On stage, Tallulah Bankhead's behaviour could be very unpredictable. On the opening night of Edward Knoblock's play *Conchita* it fell to her to make an entrance in the second act carrying a monkey – a live one. They hadn't had much time to get to know one another during rehearsals and once on stage in front of an audience the monkey started on the most disgraceful display of scene stealing. Miss Bankhead was on the point of delivering her first line when the monkey snatched her black wig, leapt from her grasp and ran with it to the footlights, where it displayed its prize gleefully to the audience. Deprived of her wig, Miss Bankhead presented a curious picture; dark and swarthy from the wig line down yet crowned with glorious golden tresses. The audience were splitting their sides. Miss Bankhead turned a cartwheel.

An attempt she made at playing Cleopatra in November 1937 was badly received by the New York critics and led to some memorable notices. John Mason Brown wrote, 'Tallulah Bankhead barged down the aisle as Cleopatra and sank.'

To Richard Watts Jr, writing in the *New York Tribune*, 'Miss Bankhead seemed more a serpent of the Swanee than the Nile'.

George Jean Nathan commented, 'Miss Bankhead played the Queen of the Nil.'

While Brooks Atkinson observed, 'The Serpent of the Nile is definitely not Miss Bankhead's dish.'

Perhaps it was just as well that Tallulah could come up with a well-turned phrase when the mood took her. When Beatrice Lillie asked enthusiastically if her friend had seen one of her earliest television broadcasts, Miss Bankhead replied, 'I just loved the close-ups. Your face looked like four yards of corduroy.' She held no illusions about herself, though, in later life. Towards the end of her career she remarked, 'They used to shoot Shirley Temple through gauze. They should photograph me through linoleum.' Of her somewhat racy reputation she said, 'I'm as pure as the driven slush.'

Sharp tongues seldom resisted the chance to raise a smile at her expense. During one of her Broadway appearances Coward's friend Alexander Woollcott, the critic, whispered to her, 'Don't look now, Tallulah, but your show's slipping.'

For Mrs Patrick Campbell, 'Watching Tallulah on stage is like watching somebody skating on thin ice. Everyone wants to be there when it breaks.'

Of the famous and incessant gravel voice Fred Keating was heard remarking, 'I've just spent an hour talking to Tallulah for a few minutes.' While Howard Dietz echoed him with the comment, 'A day away from Tallulah is like a month in the country.'

Much of this left the lady herself unaffected, particularly as theatre-goers on both sides of the Atlantic clamoured to see her (if only in confirmation of Mrs Patrick Campbell's opinion).

In the summer of 1947 she opened in a revival of *Private Lives* in Bridgeport, Connecticut, a triumphant production which toured the States for a year before opening in New York in October 1948. Her Amanda may not have emulated that of Gertrude Lawrence, but the audience loved it and Coward was well pleased when he saw the show. Many thought Tallulah Bankhead was funnier in the part than Gertie Lawrence; others saw a subtle critique of Coward's writing. As for Tallulah herself, she just soaked up the success.

Not long after opening at New York's Plymouth Theater, she found herself called on to follow the family legacy in national politics by adding her voice to the presidential campaign being fought by Harry Truman. From her dressing-room Tallulah introduced the President to a nationwide audience under the auspices of the International Ladies Garment Workers Union, telling her listeners,

There were Alabama Bankheads in one or another of the houses of Congress for sixty consecutive years. My father was Speaker of the House for four years, served with that body for twenty-five. My grandfather, John, sat in the Senate for thirteen years. My Uncle John spent twelve years of his life in the Upper House. They all died in harness. I would be outraging their memories, I would be faithless to Alabama, did I not vote for Harry S. Truman. Yes, I'm for Harry Truman, the human being. By the same token, I'm against Thomas E. Dewey, the mechanical man.

Truman was suitably grateful and after his unexpected victory sent Miss Bankhead a couple of tickets for his own 'opening' at the inauguration ceremonies. Not many of Noël Coward's leading ladies can have been so esteemed on both the political and theatrical stage.

During the Second World War, Gertrude Lawrence did her bit for the British war effort by collecting bundles for Britain when she wasn't busy on the Broadway stage. For the greater part of the war she was occupied in the hugely successful production of *Lady in the Dark*, a musical by Moss Hart, another of Coward's long-standing friends from that first trip to New York.

In all she played three Broadway seasons in the show and toured every major city in the States – her longest run. Victor Mature was in the original cast with her and he, like most of the other actors who trod the boards with Miss Lawrence, had a taste of her fun and games on stage. When she persisted in 'mugging' during his big scene Moss Hart had to have a sharp word with her, telling her to sit perfectly still while Victor Mature spoke his lines. Hart went to see the show the following night in which Miss Lawrence kept her word, but for one small detail. Just before Victor Mature started on his scene she had lit a match. Now sitting stock still, she was the focus of all eyes in the house as the flame burned slowly down towards her fingertips. Moss Hart's next instruction was that she wasn't to be allowed any extraneous props.

For a while Victor Mature got his scene back. Then Gertie went to the stage manager, Hart's brother Bernie, to say that a friend had sent her a bunch of violets and as she was going to be watching the show that night, Gertie wondered if she could have them on stage with her in a vase? Bernie Hart couldn't see any harm in this and the violets were duly placed on her desk. That night she very slowly and very deliberately ate her way through the whole vaseful!

On the war front itself Dorothy Dickson was one of the many American stars engaged in ENSA shows for the Allied forces. Coward was of course deeply involved with these all over the Middle East and later in India and the Far East, and it was for that reason that Dorothy Dickson approached him when he returned to London after an exhausting period overseas, asking him to help her open a Stage Door Canteen for all the allied troops in London. Coward seemed enthusiastic about the idea at their first chat, but later declined to appear, saying that he was honestly too worn out to be of any use.

This was a set-back for Dorothy Dickson, but she battled on, persuading other stars, financial backers and bureaucrats to support the idea and eventually got the Stage Door Canteen off the ground.

On the opening night she suffered the worst stage fright of her career which might have followed her on to face the audience if she hadn't bumped into Coward the moment she got inside. He'd been wrong to turn down her suggestion, he apologized, and was offering to do anything he could to help her project succeed. Dorothy Dickson's nerves melted away after that.

Twenty years earlier she had scored a number of West End hits as a musical comedy star in shows like *Tip-Toes, Peggy-Ann* and *The Cabaret Girl*. Later she starred in many of Ivor Novello's shows and became one of the select company invited to share his rather meagre hospitality at his house, Red Roofs.

Ivor Novello was always being ribbed for his care with money, which was in marked contrast to Gertrude Lawrence whose waywardness with her bank account was to land her in the bankruptcy court. Novello, on the other hand, installed a coin-operated telephone at Red Roofs, for the convenience of his guests and security of his pocket. Lilian Braithwaite once proudly showed Coward a brooch Novello had given her, adding teasingly, 'Ivor gave me this tiny diamond. Can you see it?'

Alfred Lunt and Lynn Fontanne were just two of Coward's friends who came to London to do their bit in the war effort. They arrived towards the end of 1943 to act in Robert Sherwood's play *There Shall Be No Night*, which the author had rewritten to set the action in the German invasion of Greece.

One night a bomb fell right next to the theatre. The stage manager immediately lowered the fire curtain, but Alfred Lunt shouted, 'Take it up, we're going on,' which the audience greeted with loud applause. Miss Fontanne had been waiting for her cue in the wings when the bomb landed. Lunt's first line when she entered was 'Are you all right, darling?' This was too much for her and she had to improvise for the next few minutes until she had collected her wits and could return to the text.

Even closer to the blast had been Terence Morgan, playing the part of their son. He had been blown right out of the theatre from where he had been standing near the stage door. Stunned and badly shaken as he was, he still made it on stage, brushing the dust from his uniform and smoothing his hair as he entered – carrying on in the best traditions of the wartime theatre!

A year later the Lunts were at the Lyric Theatre playing in *Love in Idleness* during that tense phase of the war when the Germans were counter-attacking in the Ardennes and the battle-worn troops were in great need of something to cheer them up. The weather's icy chill did nothing to improve their spirits and it was left to the fabulous Lunts to set their blood racing by playing a series of increasingly passionate love scenes. Performances like these became something of a speciality with the Lunts and one elderly lady in an audience spoke for many of the more staid members of the American theatre-going public, when she commented to a friend at the end of one rather daring scene, 'How nice to know they're married.'

An earlier appearance of the Lunts at the Lyric in May 1938 helped to popularize the theatrical phrase about the 'green umbrella' that has been associated with Alfred Lunt ever since.

They were rehearsing Giraudoux's Greek comedy *Amphitryon 38* when Alfred Lunt called the company together one day before they started work and told them that he was finding it impossible to play his part and accordingly the whole production was being cancelled! 'I can't find the green umbrella,' he concluded enigmatically and left the theatre. The rest of the cast were pretty stunned by this and maundered about the stage until Lynn Fontanne reassured them, 'Don't worry, we'll go on, and he'll find it.' The others were still baffled, but a little more hopeful and the rehearsal began.

Less than an hour later Alfred Lunt re-appeared to announce cheerfully, 'Don't worry. I've found it. We'll start again at the beginning of the act.'

According to Noël Coward, Alfred Lunt's unusual terminology for inspiration in a part stemmed from rehearsals for a production of *Pygmalion* eleven years earlier, in 1927. Apparently he was depressed at not being able to get to grips with his part as Higgins, and Lynn Fontanne suggested he might try carrying a green umbrella to see if this would help. Seemingly the umbrella did the trick and this particular aid to working into a character passed into theatrical folklore.

Coward had first met the Lunts at Laurette Taylor's home on Riverside Drive during one of her infamous Sunday evenings in the summer of 1921. The three of them were then struggling actors, but they shared dreams of success – one of these being that Coward should write a play for the three of them. In the fullness of time he did and they joined forces on 2 January 1933 at the Hannah Theater in Cleveland, Ohio for the first night of *Design for Living*; transferring to the Ethel Barrymore Theater in New York three weeks later.

The coming together of the three stars was an event eagerly anticipated by the theatrical community in the

THREE'S COMPANY

Leo	MR. REX HARRISON
Otto	MR. ANTON WALBROOK
Ernest Friedman	MR. ALAN WEBB
Gilda	MISS DIANA WYNYARD

States; glorious rows were expected. In the end it was to be sadly disillusioned. The only disagreement of consequence lasted two days and was concerned with nothing more serious than who should have which dressing-room. Contrary to popular expectation, the Lunts wanted Coward to have the star dressing-rooms as the author; he wanted them to occupy them while he took a small room upstairs. The issue was finally settled by Coward, who went to the New York store Macy's and bought a range of such beguiling furnishings for the smaller room that the Lunts eventually agreed to let him occupy it and moved into the ones Coward had always intended they should have.

On stage they each reflected similar respect for the others' performance and enjoyed experimenting with the play to see how they could improve the blocking or bring out a fresh laugh from a new piece of business.

The chemistry between Coward and Alfred Lunt in particular was operating so strongly that one night they were able to swap parts in the scene in which they both appeared drunk without the audience realizing that anything unusual was taking place. This was started by Alfred Lunt delivering one of Coward's lines. The deviation didn't make any appreciable difference to the plot as both characters were meant to be sozzled, so they switched roles completely and had great fun trying out each other's lines and im-

Design for Living, February 1939

DROWNING SORROW

Leo	MR. REX HARRISON
Otto	MR. ANTON WALBROOK

plementing little bits of business they mutually admired. They enjoyed themselves hugely in that scene and never missed a laugh. They did not get one from Lynn Fontanne.

'Nothing that either of you did in that scene was even remotely amusing!' she told them furiously in the wings before storming back to her dressing-room, leaving the two men to slink out to a movie, crestfallen.

(The film version of *Design for Living* had other changes in store – not ones that brought much pleasure to the author. 'I'm told there are three of my original lines left in the film,' Coward remarked, 'such original ones as "Pass the mustard." ')

Lynn Fontanne herself wasn't any stranger to improvising during a scene, but she preferred to give a little warning to her fellow actors. Following a Saturday matinée in New York she appeared in Coward's dressing-room full of excitement for a new idea she'd had for the last act of *Design for Living*. She'd often told Coward that she thought Gilda, whom she played, was the sort of woman whose handbag was crammed with a chaotic collection of odds and ends. Apparently she'd seen a woman at lunch that day whose own handbag was just like this. Lynn Fontanne had watched in fascination as she'd opened it and the contents had expanded out of it like a balloon. This was exactly the effect she wanted to achieve in the last act.

Coward thought it was a marvellous idea and asked when she was going to introduce it. She suggested a point in the scene when he would have his back to her. In her enthusiasm, Lynn Fontanne went on to explain that she knew a little man who'd be able to fix the spring mechanism in the bottom of the handbag to make everything bubble out. Then she was going to rehearse it and time it until she knew she had it right. And all of this was going to be achieved by the time of the evening performance.

'Do you mean to go to all that trouble,' asked Coward, 'knowing that this evening's performance of *Design for Living* is our very last together? That the engagement ends tonight?'

'What possible difference would that make?' replied Miss Fontanne.

A few years before *Design for Living* she and Alfred Lunt appeared in S.N. Behrman's play *Meteor*, which opened without any ending. The final scene was still unfinished at the time of the dress rehearsal and the director and author had become embroiled in such a heated row that they had both stormed out of the theatre without the matter being resolved. Alfred Lunt said they couldn't be expected to open without knowing how the play was going to end, only to be told that they would have to because the first night was completely sold out!

It fell to Lynn Fontanne to bring the play to its conclusion, which she did in a long telephone conversation, having told the stage manager to ring down the curtain when he heard her give as an unlikely cue the Yiddish word *schlmiel*.

That's the way the first night of *Meteor* ended in Boston. By the time they got to New York, author and director had made up their differences and a more satisfactory ending had been provided.

This was just the sort of dangerous living on the stage that Coward relished on both sides of the Atlantic.

Conversation piece

NOEL COWARD DIDN'T restrict his wit to his written work, of course. His conversation, if the dozens of anecdotes about him are to be believed, sparkled with the same brilliant quips and delightful turns of phrase that characterized his stage dialogue. So, by way of a coda, here is a selection of some of those immortal lines which confirm the Master's talent to amuse off the stage as well as on.

He left a London theatre after watching an actress give a less than convincing portrayal of Queen Victoria and commented, 'I never realized before that Albert married beneath him.'

When plans were being laid for the first of the *Night of 100 Stars* charity shows, there was considerable discussion over the title for the programme. Someone suggested, *Summer Stars*, which might have worked quite well had Coward not killed it tersely with, 'Some are not!'

He once arrived for an interview with the BBC wearing a tie of exotic – some might say garish – design, but fashioned from the most exquisite silk. In spite of Coward's protestations, the sound-man insisted on clipping his small microphone to this, with the result that every time Coward moved his head the rustling of the tie added a disconcerting background to the recording. Seeing the interview afterwards,

Coward commented to the producer, 'Ah, yes – just as I thought. My tie was far too loud.'

During a rehearsal he was conducting, the Master ran up against an actor who was continually fluffing a French phrase in one of his lines. In the end Coward asked if the man could speak French. '*Un petit peu,*' answered the actor.

'I never think that's really quite enough,' Coward told him.

When Sir Alec Guinness played opposite Simone Signoret in *Macbeth*, the first time the lady had spoken English on stage, Coward summed up the production with the remark, '*Aimez-vous Glamis?*'

Coward once found himself confronted with a leading lady who assured him that she was the sort of actress who'd be more than happy to work in rep, playing Ophelia one week and walking on with a tray the next. 'The only time you go on stage carrying a tray,' Coward told her, 'John the Baptist's head will be on it.'

During one of his New York visits, Coward ran into Lady Diana Cooper, who was also appearing on Broadway at the time in the deeply religious play, *The Miracle*. 'I saw your play, Noël, but I didn't laugh once, I'm afraid,' she told him.

'Didn't you darling?' answered Coward. 'I saw yours and simply roared.'

Gilbert Harding, the acerbic broadcaster and television personality, went to see one of Coward's plays in London, fell asleep quite early on in the first act and continued to snore loudly through the rest of the play, despite efforts to rouse him. He came to with the applause at the final curtain and, when he met Coward in the foyer afterwards, apologized profusely. 'My dear fellow, there's absolutely no need at all for you to feel guilty,' replied Coward airily. 'After all, I have never bored you half as much as you have bored me.'

He was more indulgent to his friend Alexander Woollcott, the New York critic and journalist who shared Coward's sharp wit and facility for the well-turned phrase. 'As a host at his breakfast parties,' commented Coward, 'although lacking the essential grace and fragility of an eighteenth century marquise, being as a rule unshaven and clad in insecure, egg-stained pyjamas, he managed in his own harum-scarum way to evoke a certain "salon" spirit.'

Other aspects of New York received harsher censure. While playing on Broadway once he took the apartment owned by the film star Mae Murray, a vast edifice decorated in rather flamboyant and question-able taste. When a visitor mentioned that it might have been late Renaissance, Coward quickly disabused them. 'No, early Metro-Goldwyn,' he corrected.

He had ways of dealing with over-eager fans, too. Again in New York, he found himself the centre of attention in a hotel lobby and confronted by a rather pushy woman who informed him, 'You remember me. I met you with Douglas Fairbanks.'

'Madam,' replied Coward, 'I don't even remember Douglas Fairbanks.'

Back in London he called backstage to offer words of congratulations to friends in the cast of a recently-opened play. As he left by the stage-door, one of the play-goers in the crowd asked, 'How did you like the play, Mr Coward?'

'I liked the acting enormously,' was his tactful reply, carefully avoiding mention of the piece itself which wasn't to his liking at all.

'I didn't even like the acting,' retorted his question-er, before adding, 'but who am I to argue with a self-appointed genius?'

'Precisely,' replied Coward as he stepped into his waiting car, 'who indeed?'

When news reached him that an impresario whose slow wits had never endeared him to Coward had blown his brains out, the Master's only comment was, 'He must have been a marvellously good shot.'

He held no illusions about his own plays and readily acknowledged the importance of the commercial theatre in his career. 'I have never written for the intelligentsia. Sixteen curtain calls and close on Saturday,' was his honest assessment of his work.

At the same time, he hadn't any time for pretension. Discussing a projected musical with a fellow writer, his collaborator put forward the idea that its title might reflect the musical's setting in 1911 and the political mood of the time. His suggested title was *An Enquiry Into Certain Aspects of the Dogmas of World War One* .

'Too snappy,' said Coward.

He wasn't sure about contemporary music either. 'What are the Beatles?' he enquired. 'I have never been able to understand what one beat singer is saying. Perhaps I shall fare better with four.'

And he had this piece of advice for new playwrights, 'Wise beginners of playwrights will, of course, after a little while compare their press notices with their royalties and decide that they still have a great deal to learn.'

In spite of the debt that Coward acknowledged to George Bernard Shaw, he couldn't resist a gentle dig at his old mentor when the opportunity presented itself. Nigel Patrick, with whom I played in *Present Laughter*, once asked Coward about a programme in which Lewis Casson and Sybil Thorndike were to appear in two of Coward's plays from *Tonight at 8.30* and also one by Shaw. He wanted to know what the Cassons were doing.

'Two of my plays,' replied Coward, 'and one of Shaw's. And that puts Mr Shaw in his place, doesn't it?'

Laurence Olivier came in for the same treatment when he wrote to tell Coward that he was to be created a Doctor of Letters. 'Doctor of four letters, no doubt,' remarked Coward.

With lesser figures of the modern stage Coward could be entertainingly perceptive in his criticism. 'When young I remember having a downward-looking view from the gallery of Tree and Hawtrey and I could hear every word,' he once observed. 'But now, swathed in stardom in the stalls, I find I don't hear as well as in the old days.'

He was equally critical of shortcomings in other areas of life. Dining once in a West End restaurant and struggling with the woodcock he had been served, he replied to the head waiter's obsequious question, 'I do hope, sir, that you found no shot in it', 'No . . . no, it died a natural death.'

'Trouble is,' he added, poking the bird with his knife, 'There's too much wood and not enough cock.'

After spending an uncomfortable night in a hotel in the tropics, sharing his bed with a collection of nibbling insects, he was settling his bill when the manager approached to ask, 'Excuse me, sir. Would you mind very much if I put up a sign reading "Noël Coward Slept Here"?'

'Not at all,' replied Coward, 'if you'll add one word – fitfully.'

While staying in Los Angeles once Coward was taken by friends in Beverley Hills to a nightclub which boasted as its star attraction an immensely tall and lean black dancer, who performed what might have passed as a ritual dance clad in nothing but a flimsy loin cloth. His body was coated with fire resistant powder and at the climax of his performance he set fire to himself. Flames appeared to engulf his body and his scanty covering disintegrated into a few pathetic cinders.

The night that Coward was taken to see this striking performance, the fiery dancer came so close to him that he sank back into his seat and cried in apparent alarm, 'Is there no limit to the talents of Peter Ustinov?'

He attended a very smart wedding once in the company of Richard Burton. At least two members of the Royal Family were also present, plus many members of the aristocracy. Coward and Burton were enjoying a peaceful glass of champagne on the terrace well in to the reception and after the Royal party had left when a succession of Lords, a Duke or two and a string of Honourables began trooping out for a breath of fresh air.

Coward took a sip from his glass and commented to Richard Burton, 'Here come the riff raff.'

During a visit to Paris he picked up a postcard of the Venus de Milo in the Louvre and wrote on the back to a friend, 'You see what will happen if you keep biting your nails!'

For many years Coward was closely involved with the work of the Actors' Orphanage, which used to stage a Theatrical Garden Party once a year. The venue on one occasion was the Oval cricket ground and in the course of a committee meeting planning the event it was announced that Surrey was prepared to play an exhibition cricket match as an attraction. The committee was told furthermore that this was to be an All Star side and not simply a Surrey county eleven. From the chair Coward commented, 'I see. They mean a Surrey With The Fringe On Top?'

When word reached Coward of the American actor Clifton Webb's extreme grief at the death of his aged mother, he took a characteristically pragmatic view and commented, 'Well over ninety . . . and gaga . . . it must be tough to be orphaned at seventy-two.'

When circumstances dictated he could also be the soul of discretion. Walking along the Brighton seafront once with Laurence Olivier's little son, Richard, they came across a couple of dogs copulating enthusiastically. 'What are they doing, Uncle Noël?' asked the little boy.

'The one in the front is blind,' answered Coward quick as a flash, 'and the other one is very kindly pushing it all the way to St Dunstan's.'

He could come out with one-word replies with just the same ease. To newspaper reporters who asked, 'Have you anything to say to the *Star?*' his answer was 'Twinkle!' – 'To the *Sun?*', 'Shine!' – 'To *The Times?*', 'Change!'

He loved sending telegrams too, even those with his own name at the end! He once wired a friend, 'AM BACK FROM ISTANBUL WHERE I WAS KNOWN AS ENGLISH DELIGHT'. And when Gertrude Lawrence married the American theatre manager Richard Aldrich, Coward cabled her,

DEAR MRS A. HOORAY HOORAY
AT LAST YOU ARE DEFLOWERED,
ON THIS AS EVERY OTHER DAY
I LOVE YOU, NOEL COWARD

However, he didn't always have it his own way and to deprive the Master, for once, of the last word, there's the story of the actress who religiously attended every audition for every show he staged in London. Each time she sang a few songs, never with any indication of improvement and always went away empty handed. After this had been going on for several years Coward started feeling sorry for her and determined that he would find something for her to do and eventually managed to come up with a part that matched her rather limited talents. 'I'm very happy to tell you that at last we have something for you,' he told her enthusiastically after walking from his seat to the edge of the stage to break the good news.

'Oh, no, Mr Coward,' replied the lady, 'I don't take parts, I just audition,' and swept out of the theatre with magnificent dignity!